General editor: Graham Handley MA PhD

Brodie's Notes on Willis Ha...

The Long and ~~~~~
and the Tall

John Jenkins
Lecturer in English, East Devon College

Pan Books London, Sydney and Auckland

Extracts from *The Long and the Short and the Tall* by Willis Hall are reproduced by kind permission of Harvey Una and Stephen Durbridge Ltd
© Willis Hall 1959

The eight lines of the chorus from the song 'Bless 'Em All! Bless 'Em All! (The Long and the Short and the Tall)', quoted on page 15, are reproduced by permission of EMI Music Publishing Ltd of 138–140 Charing Cross Road, London WC2H 0LD
© 1940 Keith Prowse Music Pub Co Ltd

First published 1988 by Pan Books Ltd
Cavaye Place, London SW10 9PG
9 8 7 6 5 4 3 2 1
© Pan Books Ltd 1988
ISBN 0 330 50262 X

Photoset by Rowland Phototypesetting Ltd
Bury St Edmunds, Suffolk
Printed in Great Britain by
Richard Clay Ltd
Bungay, Suffolk

This book is sold subject to the condition that it
shall not, by way of trade or otherwise, be lent, re-sold,
hired out, or otherwise circulated without the publisher's prior
consent in any form of binding or cover other than that in which
it is published and without a similar condition including this
condition being imposed on the subsequent purchaser

Contents

Preface by the general editor 5

The author and his work 9

The play and its genre 10

Title, background and plot 15

Act summaries, critical comment, textual notes and revision questions
Act 1 19
Act 2 26

Willis Hall's art in *The Long and the Short and the Tall*

The characters
Representative qualities 31, Bamforth 33, Mitchem 37, Johnstone 40, Macleish 42, Evans 44, Smith 45, Whitaker 47, Japanese prisoner 49

Themes 51

Language and style 57

Dramatic structure 60

General questions 66

Further reading 70

These Notes are based on the Hereford Plays edition of *The Long and the Short and the Tall* published by Heinemann Educational Books, but as references are given to particular acts, the Notes may be used with any edition of the play.

Preface

The intention throughout this study aid is to stimulate and guide, to encourage the reader's *involvement* in the text, to develop disciplined critical responses and a sure understanding of the main details.

Brodie's Notes provide a summary of the plot of the play or novel followed by act, scene or chapter summaries, each of which will have an accompanying critical commentary designed to emphasize the most important literary and factual details. Poems, stories or non-fiction texts will combine brief summary with critical commentary on either individual aspects or sequences of the genre being considered. Textual notes will be explanatory or critical (sometimes both), defining what is difficult or obscure on the one hand, or stressing points of character, style, plot or the technical aspects of poetry on the other. Revision questions will be set at appropriate points to test the student's careful application to the text of the prescribed book.

The second section of each of these study aids will consist of a critical examination of the author's art. This will cover such major elements as characterization, style, structure, setting, theme(s) for example in novels, plays or stories; in poetry it will deal with the types of poem, rhyme, rhythm, free verse for example, or in non-fiction with the main literary concerns of the work. The editor may choose to examine any aspect of the book being studied which he or she considers to be important. The paramount aim is to send the student back to the text. Each study aid will include a series of general questions which require detailed knowledge of the set book: the first of these questions will have notes by the editor of what *might* be included in a written answer. A short list of books considered useful as background reading for the student will be provided at the end.

The General Certificate of Secondary Education in Literature

These study aids are suitable for candidates taking the new GCSE examinations in English Literature since they provide detailed preparation for examinations in that subject as well as presenting critical ideas and commentary of major use to candidates preparing their coursework files. These aids provide a basic, individual and imaginative response to the appreciation of literature. They stimulate disciplined habits of reading, and they will assist the responsive student to analyse and to write about the texts with discrimination and insight.

Graham Handley

JAPAN AND SOUTH-EAST ASIA

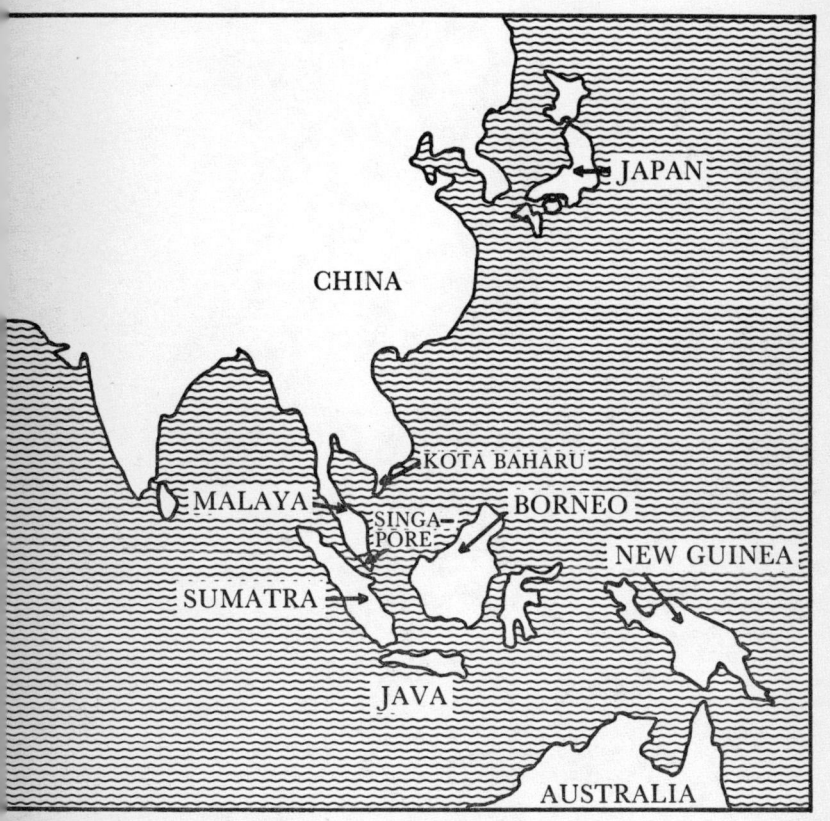

The author and his work

Willis Hall was born into a working-class background in Leeds on 6 April 1929 and educated at Cockburn High School. He served for a time in the Army and, while stationed in Singapore, wrote several pieces for Radio Malaya. Later, he was to put his knowledge of Malaya, and of life in the ranks, to good use in *The Long and the Short and the Tall*. He returned to England in the early 1950s and worked for a while as a newspaper reporter before becoming a full-time writer.

He has proved to be extraordinarily versatile and prolific in his chosen profession. He first made his name in his twenties as a writer of several successful radio and television plays. Switching to the stage, he wrote a comedy entitled *Poet and Pheasant* and then – his first stage success – *The Long and the Short and the Tall*. It opened at the Nottingham Playhouse in September 1958, was staged at the Edinburgh Festival also in that year before moving to London, where it enjoyed a long run first at the Royal Court Theatre from January 1959 and then at the New Theatre from April. Since then, his plays have included *Glimpse of the Sun* (1969), and *Crackers* (1976). He has written plays for children, too, the best known being *The Royal Astrologer* (1960), *Gentle Knight* (1967) and *The Incredible Kidnapping* (1969). A further indication of his refusal to be typecast as a writer is his authorship of several books on football, especially *A-Z of Soccer* (1970) and *Football Report* (1973).

In addition to producing books written solely by himself, he has for nearly thirty years worked with Keith Waterhouse, another working-Class North Country writer, in what has proved to be one of the most successful literary postwar collaborations. Since their first West End success – a stage adaptation of Waterhouse's immensely popular novel *Billy Liar* – they have written stage plays and screenplays, including *Whistle Down the Wind* starring Alan Bates and Hayley Mills. More recently, they have produced a remarkably successful children's television series based on a character first created by Barbara Euphan Todd, *Worzel Gummidge*.

The play and its genre

In an article published in 1954, Kenneth Tynan wrote scathingly of typical West End plays of the time:

The bare fact is that, apart from revivals and imports, there is nothing in the London theatre that one dares discuss with an intelligent man for more than five minutes . . . Our drama's prevalent *genre* [is] the Loamshire play. Its setting is a country house in what used to be called Loamshire but is now, as a heroic tribute to realism, sometimes called Berkshire. Except when someone must sneeze, or be murdered, the sun invariably shines. The inhabitants belong to a social class derived partly from romantic novels and partly from the playwright's view of the leisured life he will lead after the play is a success . . .

This stinging rebuke on the unadventurous respectability of the English stage came, in fact, right at the outset of a period when fundamental changes began to take place in the theatre as well as in the novel. New writers seemed to proliferate in number, many of them committed to challenging or at least exposing what they considered to be complacent, cosy, middle-class ideas of life. The novels of John Braine, Kingsley Amis and John Wain, and the plays of Arnold Wesker and John Osborne, for example, struck forcefully at the stifling, smug, class-ridden nature of English society by dealing instead with the passions, aspirations and disappointments of the working-class and lower middle-class. In *Room at the Top*, for instance, John Braine tells of the relentless ambition of Joe Lampton, a working-class, unprincipled young man who craves material success and elevation to middle-class status. He finally achieves it by marrying the daughter (whom he does not love) of the local rich man. By the end of the book he has discovered the hollowness of the success for which he has striven. While Joe Lampton wished for acceptance into the magic circle of middle-class respectability, the hero of another 1950s story shows a dislike of authority which is immediately recognizable in Bamforth. In Alan Sillitoe's *The Loneliness of the Long Distance Runner*, the hero, who is in Borstal, believes that as a member of the working class he cannot win in the prevailing social system, but he can at least refuse to comply with its standards. He is a magnificent cross-country runner. The governor of his Borstal wants him to win a particular race and the boy himself would like to win it. However, in order to register his defiance of authority, he deliberately loses it. Although written in a different genre, books like these bear immediate comparison with *The Long and the Short and the Tall* in their unsentimental presentation of the working class.

The same restless challenging of social and literary values was seen in the theatre also. In 1953 Samuel Beckett's play *Waiting for Godot* (written in French, translated into English by the author and so one of the 'imports' Tynan mentioned) was staged to the blank incomprehension of audiences expecting a play to have the usual ingredients of a beginning a middle and an end, some kind of narrative thrust and characters who appeared to be credible. Instead, they were presented with two tramps who are waiting for Godot. Nothing happens in the play in terms of action, the tramps talk, often repetitively and obscurely, there are long silences, Godot never comes and we never discover his identity or even if he exists at all. Yet within a decade, Beckett's work had been acclaimed a masterpiece succinctly dramatizing the hopelessness of life. His influence in liberating the theatre from the cosy notions of the well-made play was central.

Whereas Beckett is more of a philosophical than a social playwright, other younger dramatists eagerly embraced the opportunity to write plays filled with protesting, working-class voices showing the loss of direction in Britain after the war. The year 1956 proved to be a watershed in this respect because it saw the staging of a seminal post-war play, *Look Back in Anger* written by a twenty-seven-year-old called John Osborne. Although it now seems dated, even tame in its protest, its central character, Jimmy Porter, voiced the anger of the younger generation, everyone between the ages of twenty and thirty, according to Kenneth Tynan. A highly articulate, university-educated figure, Porter reacts against the genteel middle-class values that he believes suppress the expression of any energy in Britain. His sees his wife Alison, the daughter of a colonel, as typifying bourgeois apathy. Educated out of his working-class background and finding he has been fitted for no productive social role, Porter expresses resentment at traditional values, dislikes authority in the form of the colonel, is anti-religious and hostile to 'posh' newspapers because of their middle-class values. Yet he reads them because his education makes it impossible for him to be satisfied with the popular press.

Porter is designed to be a controversial character, embodying much of the frustrated energy Osborne felt lay trapped in those of working-class origin. Two years later, Willis Hall produced a character who, though obviously different from Jimmy Porter, is not without striking similarities. Unlike Porter, Bamforth has not been to university, does not find himself at odds with his background and is obviously not intended by his creator to be the voice of postwar social protest. Yet he is working class, vividly articulate (even if heavily reliant upon slang), energetic and instinctively anti-authoritarian. Porter and Bamforth have another characteristic in common; their shaky self-control easily finds expression in physical violence. This temperamental similarity is revealed in two incidents in the plays. In Act 1 of *Look Back in Anger* Porter, who has with his friend Cliff been reading extracts aloud from the quality Sunday newspapers and mocking their blandness, suddenly pushes Cliff against an ironing board and knocks it and Alison down. In Act 1 of *The Long and the Short and the Tall* Bamforth's tussle with Evans begins as nothing more than boisterous fun but becomes a means of forcing his friend into a humiliating admission. While Porter's violence is more unpredictable, the important point is that both men exhibit a restless physical energy that their volubility cannot entirely expend. It is a measure of the new direction British postwar theatre had taken, that an entire play could be written about a group of working-class soldiers, having as its central speaking role someone as crude, arrogant, yet fascinating as Bamforth.

There are two other plays that help illuminate *The Long and the Short and the Tall*, both of them taking war as their subject. They are R. C. Sherriff's *Journey's End* written in 1928, and John Arden's *Sergeant Musgrave's Dance* written in 1959. *Journey's End* offers an interesting comparison because while it is similar in structure to *The Long and the Short and the Tall* its tone, language and characters are utterly different. Set in the trenches in World War I, it reveals the tensions of a small group of soldiers in much the same way as Willis Hall's play. Like *The Long and the Short and the Tall* it is traditional in its structure, with a beginning, a middle and an end; simply drawn yet individualized characters; and is realistic within its limits. But the differences are marked, and show how much English society – and theatre – had changed in the thirty years between the composition of the two pieces. For one thing, the characters in *Journey's End* are officers and almost exclusively public-school educated. The raw recruit, Raleigh, fresh faced, idealistic and just out of his public school exudes a boyish enthusiasm that makes Whitaker's willingness to conform seem dull by comparison. Raleigh openly hero-worships Stanhope, his senior officer – who is himself only twenty-one and with whom he has been at school – eagerly telling another character called Osborne that Stanhope was not only captain of rugby, but wicket-keeper for the first eleven. Osborne, because he is older, is affectionately known as 'Uncle' by Stanhope, and this revealingly indicates the importance laid upon the close-knit cooperation under stress that was the hallmark of the officer class of the time.

The sour cynicism that is everywhere, even in Mitchem, in *The Long and the Short and the Tall* finds no place among the officers in *Journey's End*. When Stanhope has to deal with an officer called Hibbert who pretends to have neuralgia in the hope of being invalided home, he appeals openly to his better nature, urging him not to let the side down. If he is wounded, Stanhope says, he can return home and be proud of himself; if he is killed in action, then at least the misery of war will be over for him. It is a very effective piece of writing within the context of the play, but its assumption of the shared values and responsibilities of officers and gentlemen seems very remote from the rampant disaffection of Mitchem's men. Characters like Osborne are masters of understatement and restraint, refusing to allow the stress of war to make them shrill. The humour, which springs mostly from a character called Trotter (who is, revealingly, an officer from a lower social class and therefore a suitable vehicle for comedy) is often rather jolly, designed to show how brave British officers cope with danger and discomfort by laughing at them.

If *The Long and the Short and the Tall* reveals how dated the language and sentiments of *Journey's End* have become, John Arden's *Sergeant Musgrave's Dance* shows how traditional Hall's play is in its structure and presentation of its themes. Written in 1959, *Sergeant Musgrave's Dance* is set in a northern mining town, isolated by winter and divided into two camps – the striking miners, and the town council who wish to force them back to work. The exact date is not given but is generally taken to be between 1860 and 1880, at the height of British imperial power. Sergeant Musgrave and his men enter the town posing as a recruiting team. Both groups, miners and authorities, seek to use Musgrave's presence to their own advantage. In fact Musgrave and his men are deserters, and Musgrave's demented mission is to return the bones of Billy Hicks, a local boy, to his home town and demand the punishment of those people who sent him off to war. Eventually the dragoons break into the town and capture Musgrave, who is sentenced to hang – hence the play's title.

Although the play is usually set in the latter half of last century, Arden aims for greater universality by suggesting no particular historical period while evoking many. In other words, he does not attempt the 'slice of life' realism that is a feature of *The Long and the*

Short and the Tall. The play is filled with folk songs that underline the themes, and at one crucial point in the play Sergeant Musgrave breaks into a frantic dance. Obviously, Arden is working with a different idea of the theatre from Willis Hall's. It is an indication of the vitality of the English stage at the time that these two very different plays were not only written within a year or so of each other, but were actually both staged at the Royal Court Theatre in 1959.

Title, background and plot

Title

Willis Hall's original title for the play was *The Disciplines of War*. It was the director Lindsay Anderson who advised that it should be renamed *The Long and the Short and the Tall* when it opened at the Royal Court Theatre, London, in 1959. As Anderson recognized, this is a more eye-catching title for a variety of reasons: firstly, it is less off-putting than the rather abstract *The Disciplines of War*, emphasizing as it does *people* rather than ideas; secondly, the title has a more distinctive rhythm (which is hardly surprising when we remember that it is also part of the title of a song that was popular with ordinary soldiers in World War II). Thirdly, the song conveys the cynical attitude of soldiers to the discipline and hardship of military life. It also implies their feeling of fellowship for one another, united as they are in their dislike of the system. The refrain of the song goes like this:

> Bless 'em all! Bless 'em all!
> The long and the short and the tall;
> Bless all the sergeants and W.O.1s*
> Bless all the corp'rals and their blinking sons,
> 'Cos we're saying goodbye to them all,
> As back to their billets they crawl,
> You'll get no promotion this side of the ocean,
> So cheer up, my lads, bless 'em all.
>   (*Warrant Officer first class)

In other words, the subject of the song – the awfulness of army life – neatly sums up the attitude of people like Bamforth, Evans and Smith in the play. Anderson himself stated that it was the 'emotive power of popular songs' that led him to suggest the title. Fourthly, just as the song title implies that there are all sorts of people in the army, so Willis Hall's play also contains a representative cross section. Although more will be said about this later, it is worth mentioning here that the only common feature among the soldiers in the play is that they share the same social grouping – they are all working class – like the soldiers in the song.

Historical background

Even though the action of *The Long and the Short and the Tall* does not require a detailed knowledge of the events of World War II, a brief outline of some of the relevant details might help to clarify why Mitchem's patrol was in a Malayan jungle, and also explain the attitude of the British soldiers towards the Japanese.

During the period of World War II, the British government had to defend a British Empire of over 500 million people (nearly a quarter of the world's population). The two most vulnerable points of the overseas Empire were the Suez canal and the huge naval base at Singapore in Malaya. Singapore was crucial for the successful defence of not only Malaya itself (which was under British rule), but Australia and New Zealand as well. (See map p. 7). Of course, in 1939, at the outbreak of the war, the sole enemy was Germany, and a war in the Far East seemed unlikely. Nevertheless, the government had to make provision for the defence of those distant countries should it become necessary.

The necessity arose on 7 December 1941 when the Japanese landed troops on the east cost of Malaya at Kota Bharu, and in so doing signalled that they considered themselves at war with Britain. Simultaneously with the invasion of Malaya, Japanese planes bombed the American Pacific Fleet based at Pearl Harbor in Hawaii, sinking four battleships and crippling two others. As with the assault on Malaya this was done without warning and without a formal declaration of war. Indeed, at this time America was not at war with Germany either. However, on 11 December both Germany and Italy declared war on America.

Malaya was severely under-defended by the Allies at the time of the Japanese invasion. There were only about one third of the aircraft considered necessary by the chiefs of staff (senior military figures who advised the government), no tanks, and few anti-tank guns. Although the Japanese were numerically inferior, they were far better equipped than the Allies, with efficient tanks and aircraft. In fact, so inferior were the RAF's Buffalo-type aircraft against the Japanese Zeros that the RAF lost half its planes in the first day's fighting. Of the soldiers stationed in Malaya, only the 2nd Battalion of Argylls had had any serious training in jungle warfare. Because of the war with Germany, few British soldiers could be spared to defend Malaya, its protection resting principally on two poorly trained Indian divisions and an Australian division. To make matters worse, the possibility of having to fight in the impenetrable jungle seems hardly to have been considered at all by the British. The plan of defence was for the RAF and the Royal Navy to sink those enemy ships carrying troops for an invasion. The infantry – the Poor Bloody Infantry as Bamforth calls them, using that time-honoured complaint – were to man the beaches and kill any Japanese who managed to get ashore. Because they were unable to stop the Japanese landing, they found themselves instead fighting in the jungle, badly trained and with little air support. This doubtless goes some way to explain the cynical attitude to the war of virtually all the patrol members, even Mitchem, in *The Long and the Short and the Tall*.

The speed of the Japanese invasion of Malaya took everyone by surprise. No one suspected that the Japanese would be as well prepared and well equipped as they were. From the start, the Allies were fighting a losing battle. In the air the RAF pilots, undermanned and under-trained, were outmanoeuvred by their Japanese opponents. Matters were no better at sea. Britain received a further humiliation on 10 December when the battleships *Prince of Wales* and *Repulse* were sunk, with the loss of over 1,000 lives, while attempting to intercept Japanese troop carriers. The aircraft carrier *Indomitable* had been earmarked to provide protection for the battleships, but it had run aground in the Caribbean and no replacement could be found in time. Although the RAF had given the battleships what protection it could, it simply did not have the planes to cope. This meant that the ships had been virtually at the mercy of enemy bombers and submarines.

By the end of January the Japanese had captured the whole of Malaya. When one remembers that the action of *The Long and the Short and the Tall* takes place 'early in 1942' – in January, that is, only a month or so after the invasion – one realizes that Bamforth and the other conscripts have an initiation into war that is as deadly as it is sudden.

By early February the Japanese were ready to launch an offensive on Singapore itself. By mid-February it was all over: without water, petrol, and artillery ammunition, the base was forced into humiliating unconditional surrender. Winston Churchill declared it to be 'the worst disaster and largest capitulation in British history'. Taking the Malayan campaign in its entirety, over 130,000 Allied troops were lost, the vast majority becoming prisoners of war of the Japanese. The numbers of battle casualties were comparatively small on both sides: 8,000 Allied dead against 10,000 Japanese. But the families and friends of the play's characters – Smith's wife and children, the prisoner's wife and children, Evans's girlfriend, and Bamforth's twelve-year-old sister – would presumably have found this small comfort.

The Japanese attitude toward those prisoners of war deserves a mention here, partly because it is something that exercises Macleish's mind in his conversation with Mitchem early in Act 2. Rumours of acts of atrocity by the enemy abound in any war. During World War I, for example, it was commonly believed that the Germans roasted babies alive. In 1906, the Geneva Convention reached agreement on the treatment of prisoners of war. (Earlier agreements at Geneva had concerned the treatment of the sick and the wounded in war and the status of those who looked after them.) Prisoners of war should have access to food parcels from the Red Cross, rudimentary health care, and should not be tortured. However, the Japanese did not recognize the Geneva Convention, and prisoners of war who fell into their hands often suffered dismally. Part of Macleish's desire to see the prisoner as a decent sort of person is to give himself hope that the stories of Japanese maltreatment of prisoners of war are mere exaggerations.

Plot

The plot of *The Long and the Short and the Tall* is compact and straightforward. A group of British soldiers on a routine patrol, some fifteen miles from base camp and twenty miles behind their front line, take a Japanese prisoner. When they discover that the Japanese have broken through their front line, they realize that they are stranded. An argument over whether the prisoner should be killed or not leads to him being shot in a moment of panic. This alerts the other Japanese soldiers who virtually annihilate the patrol.

There is nothing to complicate this simple story. The play has no digressions, no sub-plot, no speeches expressing complex, abstract ideas and no difficult language. Its power lies in its simplicity.

Act summaries, critical commentaries, textual notes and revision questions

Act 1

Seven British soldiers on a routine patrol in the Malayan jungle take temporary refuge in a deserted storehut before beginning the fifteen-mile march back to base. Almost immediately there is a quarrel between two of them – Corporal Johnstone and Private Bamforth – which is stopped by the sergeant, Mitchem. From the outset, then, there is a sense of tension among the men, set against the larger danger from the Japanese. Mitchem and Johnstone leave the hut to check outside. The conversation among the men who remain is a mixture of banter (Evans and Bamforth), aggression (Smith, Macleish and Bamforth) and nostalgia (Evans and Smith). Bamforth is at the centre of most of the talk, whether teasing Evans or provoking Macleish. Although little is happening in terms of 'action', there are the deft presentation of character and rapid changes of mood, from humour to incipient violence, to maintain the reader's interest. Absorbed in trying to contact base on a radio with a weak battery (something that is of cumulative importance as the act develops), Whitaker takes little part in the proceedings, though he too is the subject of Bamforth's teasing. This section of the act rises to its climax when Macleish (who has been left in charge) can stand Bamforth's insubordination no longer and almost comes to blows with him. They are prevented only by the timely return of Mitchem and Johnstone.

Mitchem's fury at the behaviour of Macleish and Bamforth is that of the professional who finds enlisted men acting in an unsoldierly manner and thereby endangering the lives of everyone in the patrol. His rebuke, which is utterly justified in the circumstances, makes the reader reflect on the slipshod behaviour of the men – Whitaker apart – during the time Mitchem and Johnstone were outside.

Mitchem's intention to strike out for base is rendered more urgent by Whitaker's picking up of a Japanese transmission. Considering the weakness of his battery his reception of the signal can mean only one thing – the Japanese must be very close by. Its implication changes the course of the entire play. Whitaker and Mitchem are the first to realize that the Japanese have broken through the British front line twenty miles away and are now marching on the camp to which the patrol is returning.

With typical brisk efficiency, Mitchem prepares the men to move out, but Bamforth, on sentry duty, spots a lone Japanese soldier. Tension and humour alternate as Bamforth reports that the soldier is merely smoking a cigarette behind some cover – where he will not be caught by his officer. Mitchem orders his men to hide as the soldier, having spotted their trail, approaches the hut, but in his panic Whitaker leaves the radio on the table. This simple moment of forgetfulness has profound consequences. The soldier spots the radio, enters the hut and is seized by Johnstone who orders Evans to kill him. Neither Evans, Macleish nor Smith can do so – further evidence of their simple decency as men and weakness as soldiers. Bamforth's willingness to bayonet the Japanese is important not only because it shows his lack of sentimentality, but because it allows for a dramatic reversal of attitudes later in the play. He is prevented from bayoneting the prisoner by Mitchem's order to desist; Mitchem intends to take him back to camp so that he can be questioned.

While Smith and Macleish check that the way is clear for their departure, Bamforth entertains himself with the prisoner, speaking to him as one would to an uncomprehending child, and expressing delight when the Japanese does as he is told. The shift in Bamforth's attitude is important for it shows him beginning to respond to the prisoner as another human being rather than as an enemy. This characteristic is perhaps most evident when he actually strikes Johnstone, who is attempting to destroy the prisoner's family photographs.

Tension rises further when Smith and Macleish return to report that they have spotted massed ranks of Japanese soldiers. Virtually stranded, the men are told by Mitchem that they will wait until dark before making a desperate attempt to reach camp. Mitchem's words to Johnstone that the prisoner will have to be killed illustrate the changing fortunes of war. From being an asset, he has now become a liability. The sense of doom, which has been gathering momentum throughout this act, increases when a Japanese voice is heard on the radio uttering taunting threats in broken English.

the crickets and the bird ... song The harmony of nature provides an effective contrast with the violence of the play. Note the final stage direction of the play where, after all the human slaughter, a bird sings.

Gillo! Lacas! Lacas! Forms of Malay words, both of which mean 'Hurry up!'

stag Guard duty.

Nit Fool.

in the nick In prison.
dis. U/s Not working.
I've shot 'em I've had enough of them.
the creek without a paddle From 'up the creek without a paddle', meaning 'in trouble'.
humpy Packs.
compo packs Short for composition packs; a ration of highly nourishing food.
i/c In charge.
He'll have your guts for garters He'll punish you severely.
from haircut to breakfast time Army slang meaning every minute of the day.
toe-rag A term of general abuse.
carving up Beating up.
civvy street Civilian life.
tapes or no tapes Evans is referring to the stripes on Johnstone's uniform which signify his rank.
putting in the nut Head-butting.
Send for the cleaners To clean up the mess.
I'll take fives Odds of five to one.
Always shouting the odds Always boasting.
on the floor Fainted, presumably with embarrassment.
Taff (Or 'Taffy') a nickname for a Welshman; after the River Taff in South Wales.
Eistedfodd A Welsh cultural festival. Bamforth is mocking Evans's Welshness – as he mocks Macleish's Scottishness by calling him a 'Scotch haggis' a little later.
bints Girls.
Dodgy move A clever idea.
Straight up Honestly.
drop you one on Hit you.
Hey-jig-a-jig, . . . little pig Although this part of the chorus is not meant to have specific meaning, there is the possibility of sexual innuendo.
Henry Hall A conductor of the BBC dance orchestra, which played versions of popular tunes of the day.
We're fifteen miles . . . Marconi . . . sitting-room Bamforth's words are tragically ironic. Whitaker is, in fact, picking up a Japanese signal. Notice, too, how naturally their position – fifteen miles from base – is made clear to us. Distances play a significant role in the play. The Home Service was rather similar to the present Radio 4 though less intellectual.
doolally Substandard.
wrap up Be quiet.
to come the regimental Demand correct procedure.
Fred Karno A pre-World War I comedian, whose performance centred round acts of gross incompetence. From 1914 on, British soldiers referred to themselves rather cynically as Fred Karno's army.
giving us the heels together Command us to stand to attention.

22 The Long and the Short and the Tall

This boy Bamforth means himself. He is using London slang.
N.C.O. Noncomissioned officer.
Welsh rabbit Another instance of Bamforth mocking Evans's Welshness. He is referring to a Welsh cheese recipe. Popularly spelt 'rarebit'.
blue-house fly A bluebottle.
Two's up Let me borrow it next.
Stroll on A meaningless expression indicating impatience or exasperation.
Second Looey Second Lieutenant.
On his tod? On his own?
bedouins Arab nomads.
You wait your turn . . . two's up Another side to Bamforth's character. He wants to read the sentimental story in Evans's magazine even though he has just mocked it.
burk Fool.
creamer Mug, fool. Cockney rhyming slang: cream jug = mug.
weaning one by now She could have a child old enough to start eating solid food.
Blighty Britain.
It's a carve up It's a complete mess.
wallahs Officials.
judies Girls.
from Land's End to how's your father This slang phrase has no precise meaning, but Bamforth is being both vulgar and comic.
bull Rubbish.
snappers . . . round the drum Children running round the house.
You want to go easy, Bammo boy . . . crippled me The fight begins good humouredly, but Bamforth's high spirits are always likely to spill over into aggression.
Joan of Arc Joan of Arc (1412–1431) the historical French peasant girl who believed she heard the voices of saints calling on her to save France from English domination. Bamforth is mocking Evans who has just claimed to hear voices.
Bungy Food.
I'll swing . . . one of these days I'll kill him and be hanged for it.
N.A.A.F.I. Provisions and canteen centre administered by the Navy, Army and Air Force Institutes.
crumb Rotten.
P.B.I. Poor Bloody Infantry. A perennial complaint of infantrymen is that they have to march everywhere.
Scarpering Making a get-away.
Tin of Cherry Blossom . . . head to foot Bamforth is saying that he will disguise himself as a native by smearing himself with brown shoe polish.
whatsits Private parts.
Kew Gardens Royal Botanic Gardens in London; they contain fine specimens of tropical plants.
Tod or nothing On my own or not at all.
Tojo's boys Tojo was the Japanese Prime Minister at this time. 'Tojo'

Act 1 23

became a general name for any Japanese soldier, rather as 'Jerry' did for the Germans.
Nippos Japanese.
'Cod' American An exaggerated, unrealistic American accent.
Catterick A large army camp in Yorkshire.
The yellow peril Derogatory name for the Japanese.
the gatling's jammed A Gatling is an early form of machine gun. The line comes from *Vitai Lampada*, a famous nineteenth-century poem by Sir Henry Newbolt, in which a young officer exhorts his men to die bravely with the words, 'Play up! play up! and play the game!' Bamforth is mocking an aristocratic attitude to war more common in earlier times, which saw it as a kind of game in which one should not let the side down.
screaming ab-dabs Loss of self-control.
I'll blanco your belt . . . twopence Bamforth's offer to clean Macleish's lance corporal's white belt is of course sarcastic.
when I'm calling . . . time When I'm giving the orders.
for the high jump In serious trouble.
warning you for C.O.'s orders I'm not going to bother reporting you to the Commanding Officer for indiscipline.
with your cap and belt off While being officially disciplined, Bamforth would stand before his Commanding Officer without his cap and belt.
to put him one on See 'drop you one on', p. 21.
he'll come King's Regs He'll insist on your official punishment. King's Regulations govern a soldier's conduct.
Get fell in Stand to attention in a line.
Shower . . . That's all you are A reminder that the members of Mitchem's patrol are conscripted men rather than professional soldiers.
I'd prefer not to say Macleish has a schoolboy's distaste for telling tales.
tripes Entrails.
on fatigues Given extra duties when they return to base.
butter . . . their crutch A vulgar variant of 'butter wouldn't melt in their mouth'. Mitchem means that they come out of prison entirely reformed men.
hard-case stuff Aggressive behaviour.
barrack-room lawyer A troublemaker who uses the rules to his own advantage.
ticks Complaints.
No one else . . . pushing out signals Notice the dramatic irony. By this stage, the observant reader or spectator has begun to wonder if the signal Whitaker received was more sinister than any of the characters realize.
batt. Battery.
S.O.B. Son of a bitch – a term of abuse.
duff Substandard.
chuff the expense Regardless of cost.
geisha girls Japanese paid hostesses and entertainers.
Jalim Besar To the south of Khota Baru, where the Japanese landed their troops.

24 The Long and the Short and the Tall

ram a round apiece up your spouts Put a cartridge into the rifle breech ready for firing.
chuff your luck Curse your luck; that's just too bad.
griping Complaining.
joskins Inexperienced soldiers.
ginks Fellows (derogatory).
up to the short hairs in it A phrase that is equivalent to 'up to his neck in it', meaning 'in a great deal of trouble'.
buckshee bunch of Harries Useless bunch of men.
up to press Up to now (i.e. 'up to going to Press').
a sly swallow To smoke secretly and without permission.
nicking out the nub Stubbing out his cigarette end.
Sarge! The set! One of the pivotal points of the play. The Japanese soldier is about to turn away when he spots the radio. From Whitaker's understandable moment of forgetfulness in leaving the radio exposed, the play swings towards tragedy.
pack in ... greyhound ... bunny lark Stop behaving as if you're a greyhound about to kill a defenceless rabbit.
You speakee English? Mitchem's words show how stereotyped a view he has of the Japanese. Bamforth shortly uses the same kind of 'pantomime' English.
Compronney? Understand? Having tried 'pantomime' English, Mitchem now tries a similar kind of French, i.e. *comprenez*?
to cop To become involved with.
Jack the Ripper A notorious nineteenth-century murderer.
in a Gilbertian fashion Like a figure from a comic opera by Gilbert and Sullivan.
Rita Hayworth A glamorous Hollywood actress, who died in 1987.
Geneva Convention Signed in 1906, the Geneva Convention lays down an internationally accepted code for the treatment of prisoners of war.
Woolwich Arsenal A large army camp and armaments depot in southeast London.
put the mockers Killed.
copped Captured.
my only chick My only child.
blonce Bonce, head.
Allee lightee All right. Once more, Bamforth is mimicking the way he thinks the Japanese speak English.
loof Roof.
Happen Perhaps.
a dodgy number A risky venture.
to belt it ... out of hell To make a quick getaway.
Flingers off blonce Fingers off head.
in the cart In trouble.
stuffing my nut Worrying my head.
muckers Friends.
short in the pins Short legged.

chicos Children.
He's almost human Bamforth's patronizing words nevertheless reveal a fundamental change in his attitude towards the prisoner.
Herb Short for Herbert – a general term of abuse.
shot your load Gone too far.
They've broken . . . strength. Instead of being a possible asset the prisoner now becomes a liability.
put the kybosh on Spoilt.
sewn that up Made that secure.
put the blocks on them Stop them.
feeling that he is expected . . . in search of approbation The final stage directions of the Act constitute a fine theatrical moment. In his ignorance, the prisoner performs the one action he thinks will win approval.

Revision questions on Act 1

1 Follow the stages by which Whitaker's attempts to contact camp on the radio become of increasing significance in the scene.

2 Consider Bamforth's attitude towards (a) Evans and (b) Macleish in that part of the Act where Mitchem and Johnstone are out of the hut.

3 What kind of person does Whitaker seem to be?

4 Consider the part played by Smith in this Act.

5 What do we learn of the prisoner in this Act? What point would you say Willis Hall is making by presenting him in this way?

6 Trace Bamforth's attitude towards the Japanese, from the time he first sees him smoking a cigarette to the time the Japanese shows him a photograph of his family.

7 How do Mitchem and Johnstone differ in their attitude towards the Japanese prisoner? What does this tell you about them?

8 Give a brief account of Macleish's character.

9 Outline some of the distinctions drawn between the regular soldiers Mitchem and Johnstone and the enlisted men.

10 What part does humour play in this Act?

Act 2

Act 2 is shorter than Act 1 and moves economically and compellingly towards its conclusion. With Bamforth, Evans and Johnstone asleep, the early part of the scene is quiet in tone, consisting of a conversation between Smith and Whitaker, in which an opportunity is taken to fill out the character of Whitaker. There follows an important and lengthy discussion between Mitchem and Macleish on war and the ethics of killing. The emotional temperature of the scene rises when Mitchem informs Macleish of the necessity of killing the prisoner. Macleish's outrage at the callousness of such an act is contrasted with the cynical professionalism of Mitchem, though the opportunity is taken, too, of showing the more personal side of Mitchem's attitude to war. Throughout their conversation there is a steady rise in tension.

There follows a brief humorous interlude as Bamforth and Evans wake from their nap and joke with each other, but this quickly yields to further tension as Mitchem and Johnstone discuss between themselves who is going to kill the prisoner. Once again, there is an implied contrast between them, Mitchem, who was the dominant character in his conversation with Macleish, now appearing to be more uncertain than the brutal Johnstone. Mitchem's dislike of Johnstone, although never stated, is implied in his words to Johnstone here. By such effective use of character contrast, the dramatist is able to present the shifting attitudes of the soldiers towards the prisoner. The grim tone is sustained when Macleish discovers that the cigarette the prisoner has given him is British, and has probably been acquired by looting the British dead. The sudden fury of Evans and especially of Macleish (who had only moments before made overtures of friendship), at what is considered a despicable practice, underlines the men's volatile attitude to the prisoner. Johnstone, who tears the prisoner's photographs in his anger, is at least consistent in his attitude, having despised the Japanese from the start. Bamforth, who has stepped outside, informs them on his return that he had given the cigarettes to the prisoner. However, this provides only a temporary respite, as the prisoner's cigarette case is found to be British too. In the tense atmosphere that follows, Bamforth proves to be an impassioned champion of the Japanese. He denounces Whitaker as being a proven collector of 'the spoils of war', whereas there is no actual proof that the Japanese acquired the cigarette case by looting. In other words, every man, even a prisoner of war, is innocent until proven guilty.

Willis Hall prepares us for the build-up to the tragic climax of the play by allowing the stress of the previous few minutes to subside. There is, for example, a moment of comic relief when Evans and Smith change guard, and a touching account by Whitaker of his memories of a girl he met at a dance. Once again, it is Smith who is cast in the role of patient listener. From this moment of quiet nostalgia, events move swiftly to their conclusion. On learning that the prisoner is to be killed, Bamforth leaps to his defence, feeling outraged by such inhumanity. In a moment of fine dramatic intensity, he stands alone, as even Evans – his closest associate throughout the play – deserts him. The occasion provides a dramatic contrast to the scene in Act I when, of the conscripts, it is only Bamforth who is prepared to kill the prisoner. While Bamforth is being forcibly restrained, Whitaker, covering the prisoner with a sten gun, panics and fires a long burst, killing the Japanese. Aware that the enemy must have heard the gunfire, Mitchem orders a quick withdrawal, pausing only to make a final attempt to contact base camp. Moments later, the entire group, with the exception of Johnstone, is annihilated after a short exchange of fire with the Japanese soldiers. Their death screams provide a chilling reminder of the brutality of war. Johnstone re-enters the hut, badly wounded, in time to hear base camp responding on the radio. Sickened by the irony of it, he curses into the set, helps himself to a cigarette from the dead prisoner, waves a white flag of surrender, and waits.

a bird sings out in the jungle Once again, an effective contrast between the plight of the soldiers and the activity of the natural world around them. Whitaker's reaction shows his youth and inexperience.
They saw you coming They soon knew you could be completely fooled.
You can see . . . It gets dark A rare example of humour from Smith.
bucks Dollars.
Peruvian gold Peru, home of the Incas, was once believed to be a land of fabulous wealth.
half-inched Cockney rhyming slang for pinched, stolen.
R.S.M. The Regimental Sergeant Major is responsible for maintaining discipline among the men.
personal kit inspection The R.S.M. was empowered to inspect men's uniforms and equipment to ensure that it was in proper order. He could also inspect their belongings if someone had reported a theft.
He'd want his head looking at He would need to see a psychiatrist (for being so stupid).
gob Drink.
jacking in Surrender.
Dracula A legendary vampire, believed to suck human blood at night.

Mitchem is sarcastically suggesting that Macleish expects the enemy to look like monsters rather than men.

Mugs away . . . We're all mugs The loser starts the next game. In the more dangerous practice of war, the mugs are the fools who have joined the army.

Charlie Fool.

up the dancers Up the stairs.

copping on a weekly Getting paid each week.

Clive of India, Alexander the Great and Henry Five Robert Clive (1725–74), Alexander the Great (356–323 BC), Henry V (1387–1422); all successful generals, Clive in India, Alexander in most of the then-known world and Henry V in France.

Rudolph Valentino A handsome actor in silent films.

It's a sticky number It's a dangerous mission.

little Harries Harry, like Johnstone's 'Herb' earlier in the play, was a name used disparagingly of anyone. Mitchem, speaking of the Japanese here, means something like 'little fools'.

Do you think . . . that already? An important admission from Mitchem. There is no hatred, vengeance or sadism in his decision to kill the prisoner; there is, he believes, simply no alternative.

conshi A conscientious objector. One who, on principle, refuses to fight.

All along the road You never deviate from the rules and regulations.

You like to come . . . glory of mankind You like to pretend you have high principles.

a touch like that Action like that.

connor Food.

a shufti A look.

You wouldn't chuckle You're more right than you know.

gets my hump Makes me angry.

snouts Cigarettes.

positions himself between . . . the patrol Bamforth does precisely the same thing a few minutes later. Willis Hall is preparing us for the third and climactic occasion when Bamfort physically protects the prisoner.

I thought . . . he'd knocked them off Macleish's conflicting attitudes towards the prisoner – from the time he accepts a cigarette – show his personal confusion. He is basically a decent man at the mercy of events outside his control.

You know what thought did A reproof which has been popular since the nineteenth century. Bamforth is sarcastically implying that as Macleish is not very good at thinking, it would be better if he did not bother to think at all.

slot him Kill him.

to go the bundle Another slang term would be 'go the whole hog', i.e. strike the prisoner.

whipped Stolen.

Happen he can stick them . . . Bammo Notice the dramatic irony. Although Evans does not know it, the prisoner's fate has already been decided.

Sherlock Holmes, Charlie Chan and Sexton Blake Famous fictional detectives.
skin and blister Cockney rhyming slang for sister.
knocked off nine Nippo nippers . . . nicked a golliwog Bamforth's strength of feeling is undermined by the intrusive alliteration, which makes his statement something of a tongue-twister.
gelt Money (from the German *geld*, pronounced 'gelt', = money).
give the family the bull Spin your family a tale.
to string the fives Hit with one's fists.
Al Capone A notorious 1920s Chicago gangster.
Madame Butterfly An opera by Puccini set in Japan. Bamforth is cruelly mocking Whitaker's timidity, by saying that a Japanese lady, let alone a soldier, would be enough to frighten him.
U.J. Club Union Jack Club.
gives . . . a wide berth Notice how Whitaker's fear is suggested here, and throughout the entire Act, making his panicked shooting of the prisoner all the more credible.
You screw the pictures, Whitaker Don't concern yourself with the story. Bamforth's teasing tone is made clear by the final sentence of his speech.
butcher's Rhyming slang – butcher's hook = look.
Bramah Beautiful.
She's only seventeen . . . a bit young, do you think? Whitaker's need for reassurance here again emphasizes his youth.
Roll on the duration A common expression among soldiers meaning 'Let's hope the war ends soon and then we can get back to normal life.'
Happen be one waiting for you The dramatic irony of Smith's comment – Whitaker will never get back – together with the quiet sadness of Bamforth's song soon after, provides an effective contrast to the remorseless pace of the play as it now drives to its conclusion.
buckshees Free gifts, i.e. acts of generosity.
I'm sorry, Bamforth That Mitchem speaks in this way to Bamforth shows the distaste he feels for what must be done to the Japanese. Notice that he repeats his apology a little later.
cobbler's The end, death.
It's a bloody Nip . . . He's a man! These words of Johnstone and Bamforth respectively summarize the play's concern with the conflict between the demands of war and the claims of a common humanity. Johnstone, notice, not only uses the derogatory term Nip, but also refers to the prisoner as 'It' – as though he is an animal.
Div A Division, about 10–12,000 soldiers.
he returns the case . . . pocket An important symbolic action on Johnstone's part. It is the only act of civility he shows towards the prisoner in the entire play and underlines his angry words 'Get knotted' into the radio set: war is pointless.

Revision questions on Act 2

1 In this Act Whitaker has two lengthy conversations with Smith. What do we learn of him as a consequence?

2 Attempt a character study of Mitchem based upon his talk with Macleish.

3 Trace the various attitudes of Macleish towards the Japanese in this Act.

4 What dramatic purpose is served by having Bamforth leave the hut for a few moments?

5 How do Mitchem and Johnstone approach the necessity of killing the prisoner?

6 Consider Evans's attitude towards the prisoner in this Act.

7 How credible do you find Bamforth's defence of the prisoner over the charge of looting the cigarette case?

8 Trace the way in which the Act alternates between periods of high tension and low-key comedy and reflection.

9 Try to assess why the scene in which Bamforth seeks to protect the prisoner's life is so dramatically effective.

10 What is gained by having the characters die off stage?

Willis Hall's art in *The Long and the Short and the Tall*
The characters

Representative qualities

Just as the title of the play and the song from which it comes suggest that the army is composed of all sorts of people, so the playwright is careful to offer a cross section of personalities in the play itself in order to broaden its appeal. This cross section can be viewed from several angles. At its most obvious there is the distinction between the professional soldiers Mitchem and Johnstone and the conscripts who make up the rest of the patrol. On several occasions the regular soldiers express criticism of the general sloppiness and indiscipline of people like Bamforth, who have merely joined up for the duration of the war. Such an attitude by professionals toward 'amateurs' is instantly recognizable as a general human characteristic and is not peculiar to Mitchem and Johnstone, or to the wartime army.

The patrol is representative in other important ways, however. There is, for example, the way in which several of the characters provide geographical variety: Macleish is Scottish, Evans Welsh, Smith and Whitaker Tynesiders, Bamforth a Londoner. Each has regional or national characteristics of his own that add to the flavour of the play. Smith is the typical phlegmatic northerner; Bamforth the cheeky, sharp-witted, fast-talking cockney who knows his way round the big city; Macleish the quick-tempered Scot; Evans the chapel goer from the close-knit Welsh valleys. These regional differences come through frequently in their conversation, occasionally in the form of boasts. On the topic of fighting, for instance, Evans is proud that the toughest fights are to be found on a Saturday night in Cardiff docks. Bamforth is quick to defend his own city in this matter by saying that fights in Cardiff are what he dismissively terms country stuff compared with what happens in London. Smith, the Geordie, immediately expresses his contempt for 'Bloody southerners'. So it is important to recognize this kind of bickering for what it is: Mitchem's patrol is composed of a collection of characters from mainland Britain each of whom is proud of his own region, each of whom has been shaped and influenced by his background. Given their limited knowledge of life, they frequently see people from other regions in terms of broad stereotypes. Smith's comment above is a good example of this, but Bamforth, too, often sees Evans and Macleish as representatives of their race rather than as individuals.

Of course, Willis Hall is not the first playwright to include this kind of regional variety in a play. Shakespeare in *Henry V* did precisely the same thing. When Henry invades France, Shakespeare ensures that his officers include a Welshman (Fluellen), an Englishman (Gower) a Scot (Jamy) and an Irishman (Macmorris). His purpose is to give an image of regional differences that is rich and diverse, but subordinate to the overriding national interest of beating the French. There is no such unity or idealism in *The Long and the Short and the Tall*. Whereas Shakespeare presents the coming together of all parts of the kingdom in a grand heroic venture, Willis Hall depicts the men of Mitchem's patrol as a random sample – the long and the short and the tall – from all parts of mainland Britain, united only in cursing their luck and feeling disillusioned with their lot. In this they are embodiments of the complaints of all soldiers everywhere.

However, for the play to be successful, Willis Hall must also present his characters as convincing individuals. If they remained at the level of cardboard regional stereotypes, it would be impossible to identify with the complex and often contradictory emotions they feel during the course of the play, particularly in response to the Japanese prisoner. And it is through our identification with their predicament that the tension and the ultimate tragedy are most powerfully felt. The prisoner, too, functions as both an individual and a representative of a larger idea. He is completely individualized (think of the careful background detail we are given about his family) but at the same time Willis Hall allows us to see, through him, the more general plight of an ordinary and far from heroic man trapped in the net of war. In this the prisoner is like the conscripts who guard him.

So far, we have been principally concerned with the presentation of the characters in terms of their regional differences. But they are representative in another, more specific, way – as men living within the disciplines and practices of the army. Looked at in this way, Mitchem is the typical tough but not callous sergeant; Johnstone the ruthless violent corporal; Bamforth the insubordinate trouble-making private; Whitaker the young nervous recruit who is anxious to follow the rules; Evans the gullible provincial; Smith the reserved married man; Macleish the lance corporal who has been promoted within the group and now finds it difficult to discipline it. Once again, their success as characters depends on the playwright's ability to suggest these larger stereotypes without ever allowing the figures to become merely mouthpieces for his ideas. A measure of Willis Hall's skill is that, Johnstone apart, the characters mentioned above are more complex than those definitions suggest, each of them being given a simple but coherent individual identity, though the definitions undoubtedly reveal important and enduring aspects of each personality.

Bamforth

The barrack-room lawyer

Bamforth is the most richly presented of all the characters, a fully realized mass of contradictions, opinions and attitudes, which unite to generate a dynamic, compelling figure. He dominates virtually every conversation in which he takes part, exhibiting in the course of the play an inexhaustible eloquence, mental ingenuity and physical vigour. He has opinions on everything – what is happening at home, how to keep wives faithful, what to do when the Japanese attack – all of which are expressed in a vocabulary and tone that are unmistakably his. The critic Kenneth Tynan has said that Bamforth's character reveals 'violence beneath banter, and a soured, embarrassed goodness beneath both' (see p. 70).

The violent aspect of his character is revealed in the opening minutes of the play. He begins by being insubordinate to Johnstone, rather like a naughty schoolboy with a teacher, having a ready though implausible excuse when challenged. The excuse – that he did not say anything but merely coughed – is not meant to be believed; it is designed purely to provoke Johnstone. So Bamforth's dislike of authority is immediately established. It is quickly followed by his willingness to translate this dislike into physical action. Only Mitchem, who crosses to intervene, prevents a fight breaking out.

While Mitchem and Johnstone are absent on a sortie, Willis Hall takes the opportunity to consolidate aspects of Bamforth's personality that have been already revealed, and to introduce new ones. His background, the slums of London, indicate why he is quick-thinking, violent, and anti-authority. In Bamforth's world one can only rely on oneself. Any rules and regulations, especially King's Regulations, exist to be used for one's own purpose, but have no other value. Bamforth knows his rights and is quick to assert them; he is equally quick to undermine the rights of people he dislikes, especially Macleish and Whitaker because they take their responsibilities seriously. He gains immense pleasure in provoking those with responsibility, driving Macleish, for example, to the point of violence by his mockery and insubordination. The enjoyment he derives from trying to make Macleish fight him is twofold. Firstly, there is the pleasure of the fight itself. Secondly, Macleish is proud of being a lance corporal but would be demoted for striking a fellow soldier, and this humiliation would give Bamforth satisfaction.

But he is far more than the aggressive slum dweller so far suggested. His teasing can be cruel, but it can also be good-natured; it is especially so with Evans, who takes his banter in the spirit in which it is intended. Even his jokes about the Scots, for example, are not malicious; he does the same thing with Evans about the Welsh. But Macleish takes them as personal insults. Another important aspect of Bamforth is revealed in the incident with Evans's magazine. The sentimental serial Evans is following provides Bamforth with a rich source of humour, yet he insists on reading it when Evans has finished. While he would claim to find the improbable events hilarious rather than moving, there is the suggestion of a more sensitive personality, which exists alongside his tougher, more aggressive nature. His fight with Evans shows yet another side of his character. It starts off as nothing more than boisterous high spirits. But Evans's refusal to submit brings out the incipient violence that always lurks just beneath the surface in Bamforth's character. It brings out something else too: single-mindedness of purpose, which shows itself on a much graver occasion in Act 2. So by the time Mitchem and Johnstone return, Willis Hall has firmly placed Bamforth at the centre of the stage. His rebellious refusal to conform to army life, his volatile nature and willingness to speak his mind are all features Willis Hall develops in subsequent scenes in the play. What emerges too is that Bamforth is ignorant of vital areas of his own personality. In telling Smith confidently that 'it's going to be every man for himself' when the time comes, there is no doubt that he believes it; however, events prove him wrong.

It is his relationship with the prisoner which clarifies and magnifies his character. His reaction on seeing the Japanese enjoying a quick cigarette is important because of its spontaneity. In speaking as he feels, Bamforth speaks the truth. To call the Japanese soldier a 'crafty old Nip' and a 'skiving get' (nowadays the word would be 'git') shows Bamforth responding to a fellow shirker. For a brief moment, the Japanese is just another soldier, not an enemy. Bamforth's attitude here can be contrasted with Mitchem's sour words immediately after. While Bamforth is laughing at what he considers a humorous inci-

The characters

dent, Mitchem is thinking of the more serious implications. Of course, this laughter does not stop Bamforth from raising his rifle to shoot the Japanese or offering to bayonet him a little later. Bamforth is no sentimentalist, and certainly no idealist, but the incident helps us to accept the relationship that later springs up between Bamforth and the prisoner.

At no time does Bamforth's attitude towards the prisoner stem from some high-principled notion such as brotherly love or universal justice. Bamforth has no time for abstract notions at all. He begins by treating the prisoner as a rather backward child, or even a pet that can be trained to perform to order. His condescending attitude towards him only changes in the final crisis, when he acknowledges that the Japanese is a man too. Initially, the prisoner provides some welcome entertainment for him. The grotesque English that Bamforth uses is merely a more dramatic variation of his inclination to stereotype the Japanese as he has already stereotyped Evans as a Welshman and Macleish as a Scot. Gradually, however, his attitude changes. His comment 'You're as bad as Smudge' on being shown a photograph of the prisoner's family marks an important step forward because it shows Bamforth responding to the man's humanity, not his nationality. This changing response is shown in more stark form when he hits Johnstone, who attempts to tear the prisoner's photographs. The violence of the attack is a timely reminder that Bamforth is no faint-heart but, more importantly, it shows him siding with the enemy over what he considers to be an affront to basic human decency. Of course, Bamforth would have no patience with such lofty sentiments when put in a generalized form. He responds to the man and the occasion, not to the idea.

By the end of Act 1 we have all the information we need to understand Bamforth's character. He is cynical, crude, provocative, arrogant, boastful, aggressive, and unwilling to toe the line. But he has also shown a sense of humour and a quick wit (his pun on 'relieve', for example, when he recounts how the General asked him to go to Malaya to relieve the situation and 'before I had time to relieve myself, here I was'). This is not all, though, for there is also his ability to strike up friendships, not only with Evans, but with the prisoner too, and a rough sense of justice, which is more powerful than he yet realizes.

Act 2 further extends his character. We see less of the humorous Bamforth as Willis Hall develops the darker tensions in the play. But it is completely credible that of all the soldiers it is Bamforth who would give the prisoner some cigarettes. His contempt for army 'red tape', (except when it suits him) has been made clear in Act 1 and he quickly dismisses Johnstone's protest that prisoners should not be given cigarettes. Similarly, his eloquent defence in the matter of the cigarette case shows a concern for justice that is developing rapidly. This concern means that he feels no special loyalty to his group. Just as he has assaulted Johnstone a little earlier, so he now humiliates Whitaker. He convinces no one absolutely of his case, not even the reader, but his words prepare us for his more dramatic defence of the prisoner in a moment or two.

Just in case there is any inclination for the reader to have a rather idealized picture of Bamforth at this stage, Willis Hall inserts an exchange of words between him and Whitaker that shows the cruel mockery of which Bamforth is capable. Whereas his exposure of Whitaker's collection of Japanese mascots can be understood as part of his defence of the prisoner, his ridiculing of the young man's sexual inexperience is more cruelly motivated. Bamforth can unerringly spot the weaknesses in a character (as he does with Macleish) and exploit them mercilessly. So it is impossible to see Bamforth simply as a noble, idealized figure, standing for the sanctity of human life. He evokes a more ambiguous and disturbing response. His violence and remorseless arrogance chill the warmth of our feelings; yet we are irresistibly drawn to his unshakeable self-confidence and crudely expressed sense of what is right.

This is felt most powerfully when Bamforth alone argues that the prisoner should not be killed. His voice is the voice of broad humanity speaking out against the cruel dictates of war. His argument that the Japanese has done nothing to them, and therefore should not be killed, strikes the reader at once both by its truth and its impracticality in the circumstances. It is only when he is under this intense pressure that he expresses his simple opinion of the Japanese – that he's a man. This is an important admission from Bamforth for, as we have seen, his attitude towards the prisoner up to this point has been condescending. All that has changed. His words to Mitchem 'It's him and me' show that Bamforth regards the prisoner not as a racial stereotype, not as a plaything, not even as an enemy, but as another human being.

When Smith asks to be left out of it, Bamforth's harsh response of 'You're in it up to here' is a crudely worded but exact echo of the words of John Donne, a sixteenth-century poet and clergyman, who wrote:

No man is an island, entire of itself; every man is a piece of the continent, a part of the main . . . any man's death diminishes me because I am involved in Mankind; and therefore never send to know for whom the bell tolls; it tolls for thee.

Just by being alive, Donne says, we're 'in it up to here'. For much of the play Bamforth would doubtless have mocked this idea in the way he mocks everything else. But when the most crucial decision of all has to be made, he sides with Donne and humanity.

Mitchem

I'm not a thinking kind of man

Mitchem is a regular soldier, tough and ruthless but not inhuman. Within minutes of the play's opening, he gives clear indication of his capabilities: stopping the quarrel between Johnstone and Bamforth; organizing the sentries; checking with the wireless operator; informing his men how long they will be staying in the hut; then leaving with Johnstone to check outside. When he returns to find Macleish preparing for a fight, his anger is that of the military professional in the face of sloppy and, in the circumstances, dangerous behaviour. Even here, his military training does not desert him. When he orders his men to fall into line before him, he does not forget to tell Johnstone to stand guard at the door. There is no personal animosity in his rage. He is not concerned with using his rank to settle scores, as Johnstone is with Bamforth, but with giving a well-deserved rebuke. To this end, he displays a gift for biting sarcasm when he ridicules Macleish's refusal to name his opponent with 'Please, Miss, it was Jimmie Smith who sat on the tomato sandwiches but I promised not to tell', and no less a gift for the blunt but vivid image. This tough, uncompromising attitude is also evident when he reprimands Bamforth a little later. It is noticeable that at no point does Bamforth, who is generally never short of words, try to interrupt.

So far there has been little attempt to individualize Mitchem; the qualities he has shown are those of virtually any army sergeant. But after the incident with Bamforth, Willis Hall begins to deepen his character, so that a sense of the individual man emerges alongside the professional soldier. When Johnstone sarcastically belittles Whitaker's skill as a radio operator, Mitchem quietly, but firmly, defends him saying that it is not his fault. Then, moments later, he shows his practical turn of mind. While Johnstone is fulminating against whoever is responsible for issuing them with a faulty battery,

Mitchem's more restrained view is that it is futile to be angry when nothing can be done. This determination to keep everything in proportion, and most of all not to lose self-control, is a feature of his personality more deeply probed in Act 2.

Along with Whitaker, Mitchem is the first to understand the significance of the Japanese radio operator's voice, and immediately takes control. Under pressure now, he is swift to silence Macleish who is worried about his brother. This is not callousness, but the same practical attitude he has already displayed. Whatever has happened to Macleish's brother is irrelevant, given the sudden danger of their own position. In another long speech (the two longest speeches in the entire play are his) he faces up to that danger. Aware of the panic around him, he speaks with the voice of common sense, calming but not deluding. If the Japanese have broken through in strength then he and his group have no chance of escape. However, Whitaker might have simply made contact with a Japanese patrol, which is now as frightened as they are. His words are not designed to be soothing – he voices his low opinion of his men frequently in this speech – but to crush their panic and offer a realistic view of the possibilities.

His decision to take the prisoner back to base is a controversial one, and in the event an unwise one, but it comes from a larger conception of his responsibilities than, say, Johnstone has. He has no wish to satisfy a primitive bloodlust by killing the prisoner. On the contrary, he immediately sees that the prisoner might be of use in providing invaluable data on enemy numbers, artillery and positions. For Mitchem, attempting to take the Japanese back to base is worth the risk for the value he might have for the British army as a whole. This sense of responsibility towards the army he serves rather than merely to his patrol is evident again when, just before the end of Act 1, he instructs Whitaker to try to contact base with the news that the Japanese have broken through the front line. Whitaker is quick to point out the danger of such an action. Mitchem is equally quick to tell him to persevere. For Mitchem, it is essential that base is informed even if doing so allows the enemy to pinpoint their position in the hut.

His long conversation with Macleish early in Act 2 is vital for a full understanding of Mitchem's character. He is quick to perceive that Macleish's horror on being told that the prisoner must die comes not so much from the moral outrageMacleish voices as from cowardice. Yet Mitchem is not generally a vindictive man. He is not, for instance, filled with a consuming hatred of the Japanese. When he tells Macleish that most of the enemy are poor fools in much the same way as the British soldiers are and, like them, have no idea of what they are fighting for, he is expressing what he feels is a perfectly obvious viewpoint. Experience has taught him, however, that all men are capable of killing each other, and sadly this means there will always be wars. He apportions a large part of the blame to women, who induce men to join the army out of bravado. This cynical attitude towards women is interesting, for we are told nothing of Mitchem's private life, and the inference is that he does not have one. Curiously, in this sequence with Macleish, he seems to have more sympathy for the ordinary enemy soldier than he does for women, who seem to be no more than troublemakers, urging a man to join up, and when he is dead finding another to take his place.

The notion of battle as a glorious activity, filled with heroism and high ideals is alien to Mitchem's sour view of war. The reality of conflict is what they are experiencing in the hut, trapped with a prisoner they must kill. Mitchem concedes to Macleish that it is murder, and goes further, to express his disgust at the entire business of war. But when he says, 'So what am I supposed to do? Turn conshi? Jack it in? Leave the world to his lot?', he is revealing once more his simple sense of responsibility and duty. In this respect he is, curiously, most like Bamforth, although vastly different from him in every other conceivable way. In the final tense moments of the play, Bamforth's stance shows him acting from a sense of duty to basic but universal humanitarian principles as personified in the defenceless prisoner. There is no shirking this duty; to be alive is to be burdened with it. Similarly, Mitchem feels it is his duty to defend the way of life he knows and values against the alien and despised traditions of the enemy, whoever they may be. It is not a task he relishes. He feels he simply has no choice; pacifism would be no alternative. Perhaps this explains why he twice apologizes to Bamforth, firstly when telling him not to give the prisoner any more water (it was Mitchem himself who saw to it that the prisoner had a drink earlier), and secondly when Bamforth learns that the prisoner is to be killed. Saying sorry is not something Mitchem finds easy, and certainly not to Bamforth whom he has already had occasion to reprimand. So this apology offers an important insight into his character. He glimpses in Bamforth something he had no idea was there, and his apology is an acknowledgement from one man of responsibility to another.

However, Mitchem is no idealized portrait of a soldier. It is the contradictions in his character that bring him to life. He is as capable of showing hesitancy in his conversation with Johnstone over who should kill the prisoner as he is of striking violently from the prisoner's hand a cigarette case he believes has been looted. Although he does not claim to be a thinking man, he has evidently reached certain conclusions about the violence inherent in men, the way they are easily misled by women into joining the army, and the utter brutality of war. Yet he remains a professional soldier to the end. Virtually his last action before leaving the hut is to tell Johnstone to make one final desperate attempt to contact base even though they themselves have no chance of escape.

Johnstone

I'd like to ram his pig-muck battery down his throat

Johnstone is a violent sadistic man who finds in war the opportunity to behave in a way unacceptable in civilized society. He is the most simply presented, consistent character in the play. Whereas all of the others have redeeming qualities to counterbalance their weaknesses or vices, Johnstone has none. Like Mitchem he is ruthless, but unlike Mitchem his ruthlessness reveals itself in personal vendettas against those he dislikes. His hounding of Bamforth is an example of this. Whereas Mitchem can control Bamforth by verbal abuse when it is necessary, Johnstone invariably resorts to the threat of physical violence. This comes partly from a failure to make Bamforth respond in any other way, which itself tells the reader something very important about Johnstone: he has little natural authority, relying on threats of brutality to impose his will.

Johnstone thrives on conflict in a way that Mitchem does not. The difference in the two men is suggested just after the patrol has entered the hut. On being told by Mitchem to organize a sentry rota, Johnstone selects Bamforth. When Bamforth makes some insubordinate remarks Mitchem merely tells him to watch it. But Johnstone is unable to control himself, launching into a series of threats to Bamforth, whose cool replies inflame him further. Mitchem has to intercede to stop them. The point here is that Johnstone is more concerned with his quarrel than he is with instructing Bamforth to do his sentry duty. Easily aroused and quick to threaten, Johnstone fails to put his personal dislike of Bamforth behind the more immediate need to post sentries. It is something Mitchem would never do.

The savagery of Johnstone is most clearly shown in the way he treats the prisoner. Before that happens Willis Hall provides two comparatively minor but revealing incidents that further clarify

Johnstone's character; he is revealed as being a man filled with anger, forever looking for someone or something on which to vent it. The first, his comment to Whitaker 'How much a week do they pay you for this, lad?' when Whitaker is having difficulty with his radio, is a characteristically spiteful comment, thrown into relief by the sensible moderate words of Mitchem. The second incident follows shortly after, when he says what he would like to do to the man who issued them with a substandard battery. His violent words reflect his violent nature, and are all the more noteworthy because his anger is pointless in the circumstances; there is nothing he can do about it until he returns to base.

So, in his quarrel with Bamforth at the outset of the play, and his boiling, but useless, rage at whoever issued the battery, Johnstone has shown how little self-control he has and how something that affects him at the moment blots out any understanding of other and perhaps larger concerns. This characteristic shapes his opinion of war, which for Johnstone is synonymous with killing; there is nothing more to it than that. He ridicules Macleish's defence of the Geneva Convention on the rights of prisoners of war because in a war prisoners should have no rights; not even the right to life. Nor can he understand Mitchem's reasons for sparing the prisoner because of any useful information he might be able to provide. Immediate gratification of a primitive instinct to kill is more important to him than any idealism or pragmatic responsibility to those who might benefit from what the prisoner can tell them.

Frustrated in his wish to have the prisoner killed, he ensures that the Japanese receives no comfort or civility from him. When he learns that Macleish has accepted a cigarette from the prisoner he asks crudely whether it is because Macleish fancies him. Virtually every aspect of Johnstone's behaviour is designed to frighten or humiliate the prisoner. He first of all tells Bamforth to throw away the prisoner's wallet; then, in an act of studied sadism, offers the prisoner a light only to strike the cigarette from his lips at the last moment. Seconds later he grabs the prisoner with the intention of destroying his photographs. When he finally tears the photographs, later in Act 2, he does so slowly and deliberately in front of the prisoner, revelling in his power. It is a telling act on his part, for it confirms he is something other than merely a violent man. After all, Bamforth can be violent, too, and in the belief that the Japanese is a looter even Macleish forgets his ideals and strikes him. But Johnstone's action is more calculated than Macleish's, showing him to be a true sadist: someone who takes a perverted delight in inflicting pain for its own sake. When he and Mitchem discuss in Act 2 who will kill the prisoner, Mitchem's reluctance contrasts with Johnstone's willingness. Even Mitchem senses that bayoneting the prisoner would actually give Johnstone pleasure.

At the end of the play, with the rest of the patrol dead, Johnstone is presented less critically by Willis Hall. His angry words to base camp are understandable in the circumstances, though one suspects that Mitchem would have warned of the Japanese advance. But it is his actions that are more important than his words in the closing moments. Returning the prisoner's cigarette case after helping himself to a cigarette is the only non-hostile gesture he makes towards him in the entire play. It is as if he now glimpses the futility of it all. He waves the white flag not because he is a coward, but because by being a prisoner he might hinder the Japanese advance. However, if the Japanese have soldiers like Johnstone in their ranks his chances of living long enough to do so are slight.

Macleish

I feel it's my duty to back up my fellow N.C.O.s

Having recently been promoted to lance corporal, Macleish is determined to act in accordance with the responsibilities of his new rank. He takes himself very seriously, perhaps too seriously on occasions. His speech to Bamforth, for example, from which the above quotation is taken, borders on the comic because of its awkward, self-important tone. He is obviously aware that having accepted a promotion he might be seen by his former associates as a toady, someone who is keen to please those in authority. So he is caught in the middle—no longer merely one of the men, but not someone with much authority over them either. This makes his position difficult to maintain, especially with someone like Bamforth, whose attitude at the best of times is insubordinate. Even the usually genial Evans reminds him that before his promotion he complained about Johnstone as much as they did.

He is hampered, too, by his sensitivity to jokes about the Scots. Bamforth's references to him as a 'Scotch haggis', a 'haggis basher' and to the 'Jocks' in the jungle screaming for 'women, beer and haggis' are merely part of his general repertoire of insults, in the same way that he insults the Welsh through Evans. But Macleish is inflamed by the 'jokes'. The row between Bamforth and Macleish in

Act 1 originates from these two characteristics of Macleish: his difficulty in asserting his authority, and his quick anger at jokes about the Scots. When confronted by Mitchem his reluctance to inform on Bamforth once again shows his uneasy divided loyalty.

So far in the play his character has been sketched in without being individualized to any degree. As further details emerge Macleish becomes a more rounded figure. There is, for example, the genuine concern for his nineteen-year-old brother who has recently been sent to the front line. When it becomes clear that the Japanese have broken through that line, Macleish's worries become graver because he is ignorant of his brother's fate. It is impossible not to feel sympathy for him here. Then there is his belief in the rules governing the conduct of prisoners, which hints at a basic human decency. He argues with Johnstone in Act 1 over whether it would be right to kill the prisoner. But this idealism is shown to be superficial in Act 2 when he is subjected to greater personal strain.

Macleish's long conversation with Mitchem in the early stages of the second act deepens his character by exposing some of the suspect, though understandable, views he holds. His complete inexperience of war becomes apparent too. There has already been one glaring example of it in Act 1, when he allowed himself to be drawn into a quarrel with Bamforth, thereby leaving the hut inadequately guarded. Now he becomes the subject of more searching scrutiny. He bases his hope that the Japanese treat their prisoners reasonably well on the fact that the prisoner seems to a fairly ordinary type of man. As his brother might already be a Japanese prisoner of war, his need to believe this is quite understandable, but it is nonetheless an obvious delusion. As the conversation develops, the reasons for his belief in the rules of combat also come under examination. Mitchem scoffs at Macleish's repugnance at killing the prisoner because he suspects it is being used as a convenient cloak to hide his reluctance to face up to the cruel necessity of war. Mitchem is proved to be right in his assessment of Macleish, but this is not to say that Macleish is a hypocrite; he is merely ignorant of his own character and feelings.

His personal confusion is seen in the incident with the cigarette. It begins quite touchingly with Macleish trying to establish a relationship with the prisoner. When we remember that Macleish's brother might be dead or a Japanese prisoner of war, this action in itself shows him to be not usually of a vindictive nature. However, when he learns that the cigarette is a British one, all thoughts of the Geneva Convention vanish, to be replaced by a primitive desire for revenge. Macleish discovers here the unsavoury truth, that the practice of war makes it difficult to reconcile what one believes to be right with what one finds oneself doing in the heat of the moment. Although he shamefacedly picks up the cigarette case for the Japanese, he fails the final acid test. When called upon by Bamforth to support his defence of the prisoner, Macleish stares out of the window, his back to Bamforth, letting his silence speak for him. Macleish is an ordinary man who believes the ideals he holds to be sincerely held. The savage experiences he undergoes show that they cannot withstand the pressure of war.

Evans

I can't! I can't. Corp, I can't

Evans is Bamforth's closest associate in the play. Although he is the object of much of Bamforth's humour, he is too good natured to take offence at it. Perhaps he admires Bamforth's quick wit and worldly knowledge to the extent that he is willing to be the butt of his jokes if he can also be his friend. Very early in Act 1, when Bamforth is explaining precisely how he would conduct himself in a fight with Johnstone, Evans asks him if he would really fight that way. This is the first indication of two of Evans's most noticeable characteristics – his naivety and his sense of what is right (one realizes from his tone that he really disapproves of such fighting).

Unlike Bamforth, Evans's experience of life has been extremely limited and he is likely to believe anything that Bamforth tells him. Bamforth's preposterous 'Margaret Denning' letter, which supposedly advises the Welsh girl to marry a private rather than a corporal, has Evans unsure for a moment as to whether it is true. This leads him on to express his views about premarital sex. Although Bamforth laughs at him, the matter has clearly exercised Evans's mind in a serious way. He has already said that he is a regular chapel goer. Even if he is not being entirely serious it is clear that the chapel, with its central position in Welsh valley life, has strongly influenced his moral outlook. This poses the question why he should value the friendship of someone like Bamforth who is so different from him in personality, background and values. The answer seems to be that, although Evans has no wish to escape from being the kind of person he is, he can taste and enjoy the excitement that he feels a Londoner like Bamforth creates. In other words, he likes Bamforth because Bamforth seems to be everything he is not.

The characters

By nature Evans is a home-loving, conventional person who comes from a close-knit community. Even his girlfriend is the daughter of his mother's friend, and this shows both how strongly his own family has influenced him, and how little experience he has of the world at large. He unashamedly envies Smith his married life and yearns for exactly that kind of simple, settled existence himself. Evans is a romantic at heart, as his interest in the sentimental women's magazine story shows. The story gives a glamorous account of love and heroism in war, which satisfies his imagination though there is no evidence that he yearns for such a life himself. In other words, Evans is not a soldier, a man of action, at all. He has no desire for a dangerous and varied career and, with the exception of Whitaker, is the least suited of all the patrol members for such a life. He is even the slowest to realize the immediate danger they are in when Whitaker picks up the voice of the Japanese radio operator.

When ordered to kill the prisoner, Evans displays his military ineptitude by aiming his rifle at the prisoner, quite unaware that a gunshot would kill Johnstone as well at such close range. When ordered to use his bayonet Evans cannot force himself to do it. It is the most critical point in his life so far; the moment when he comes face to face with the reality of war as opposed to the fictional version he has encountered in his magazine stories. After this traumatic experience, Evans does not feature greatly in the rest of the first Act. Early in the second there is evidence that he has recovered some of his usual good spirits for, on waking, he jokes with Bamforth. Later, as the tension rises once more, we see how events are spiralling beyond his control. Like Macleish, he is quick to believe that the prisoner has been looting, and quick to demand punishment. He is equally quick to feel remorse when he learns that the prisoner had been given the cigarettes by Bamforth. When put to the most crucial test of all, he lacks the moral courage to stand by Bamforth and vote that the prisoner should live. This does not make him an evil man, but his weakness is exposed by the flimsy reason he gives to justify the killing of a man he could not kill himself – 'You never know about that fag case, do you, son?'

Smith

I just take orders. I just do as I'm told. I just plod on

Smith is a Tynesider, a 'Geordie', and has all of the northerner's scorn for the southerner. He impatiently dimisses Bamforth's claims about

London street fighters, remarking that southerners do little else but boast. But scorn and impatience are untypical of Smith, and he certainly holds no malice against Bamforth. His most important characteristics are level-headedness and a willingness to listen, especially to young Whitaker who is a Tynesider himself. He has none of Bamforth's intense dislike of authority and understands the awkwardness Macleish feels at having recently been promoted to lance corporal. When Bamforth starts taunting Macleish in Act 1, shortly after Mitchem and Johnstone have exited, it is Smith who tells Macleish to take no notice, and a little later tells Evans, too, to let the matter drop. His dislike of anger and argument becomes more apparent when the hostility between Macleish and Bamforth flares up again. He physically restrains Macleish, even calling him a 'dim Scotch crone', because he can see that if Macleish is drawn into a fight he will be demoted, and this will give Bamforth immense satisfaction. Smith, then, is seen early as a conciliator. However, he is no less cynical about the army than anyone else. He tells Evans that the only reason they are on the patrol is that their colonel wishes to keep them out of the N.A.A.F.I. bar. If it is true that this routine patrol is merely their commanding officer's way of maintaining morale, then their death is all the more tragically unnecessary.

Although he gets on well with the other men, Smith is a far quieter, more reserved individual than any of the others, with the exception of Whitaker. He engages in none of the schoolboy horseplay of Bamforth and Evans, and when he speaks keeps his words to a minimum. His more mature behaviour is perhaps the result of his being a married man with two children. Although not in the least articulate, he speaks movingly of his house on the new estate and his garden. Evans, who wishes for just such domestic security, understands how it must be harder for Smith to cope than it is for the rest of them. It is noticeable that Mitchem selects him to accompany Macleish on a brief reconnaissance after the prisoner has been taken, as if in acknowledgement of Smith's reliability and greater maturity.

In Act 2 another side to his character emerges, completely in keeping with what we know of him so far. He is a patient, sympathetic listener. The conversation he has with Whitaker in the opening minutes of the Act is important, not for what he says but for the reassurance he offers to Whitaker merely by listening. His criticism of Whitaker for being taken in by whoever sold him his watch is gentle, not abrasive; and his joke that you can see when it's night because it gets dark is not designed to humiliate Whitaker in the way that many of Bamforth's jokes are. It might almost be a father making gentle fun of his son. The same tone is established later when he listens to Whitaker talking of Mary Pearson. Although the comfort and hope Smith offers are uttered with characteristic brevity, what is important here is his sympathetic understanding of Whitaker's need to talk because he is afraid.

Decent a man though Smith is, he lacks the capacity for moral outrage that Bamforth discovers in himself. He is, as he implies, a plodding fellow, not especially imaginative, dynamic or given to taking initiatives. When he has to decide between his own family and that of the prisoner, he makes the selfish though understandable choice.

Whitaker

The boy who has a nervous breakdown at the thought of Madame Butterfly

Whitaker's character is established in Act 1, as much by what he does and what others (Bamforth especially) say about him, as by what he actually says himself. It is noticeable, for instance, that whereas the other men sit thankfully on the table shortly after entering the hut, and Bamforth even lies down, Whitaker immediately sets up his radio and tries to contact base. Young and keen to please, he takes his duties seriously and this makes him an obvious target for the sarcasm of Bamforth, who accuses him of being after a lance corporal's stripe. His unquestioning acceptance of army rules is even more noticeable when he is seen darning his socks for the kit inspection on Saturday. While Bamforth's response to this is predictable, we learn a little later that even Mitchem intends taking a weekend off and missing the inspection. The inference is that Whitaker is inexperienced in the ways of army life and follows the regulations unquestioningly. Not only is he diligent, there is the merest suggestion that he is the most nervous of the patrol members. It is Bamforth who first alludes to this when he jokes about the invading Japanese carving chunks out of Private Whitaker, and follows it by asking Whitaker if he is getting windy. That Bamforth should ask this question, given his acute understanding of others' weaknesses, is indication enough at this stage. The characteristic is introduced but not embellished; we note it, but do not dwell upon it. It becomes of increasing importance, however, once the Japanese signal has been picked up.

Despite this, in the first half of Act 1, Whitaker's character is subordinated to his function as a radio operator. His announcements that he is picking up a signal are peppered throughout this part of the Act and gain in sinister implication as the Act proceeds. At first, in the absence of Mitchem and Johnstone, his announcements are disregarded, but culminate in the eerie voice of the Japanese radio operator breaking the expectant silence of the hut. It is a chilling moment in the play and something that has been achieved by Whitaker's persistent devotion to duty. From now on, his function as a radio operator is superseded by his human reaction to events, though he is revealed to us principally through his actions.

Whitaker's terrified response to the Japanese voice is more important than anything he says; suddenly our knowledge of his nervousness, which has been dormant for a while, is reawakened. He is so frightened that he is incapable of speech, merely staring in blank terror at the radio set from which the voice has issued. From this point on we are never allowed to forget this trait. Willis Hall gives two further examples of Whitaker's extreme fear in the first Act, for it is this aspect of his character that is to have the gravest repercussions in Act 2. The first example occurs when the Japanese soldier approaches the hut. Mitchem orders Whitaker to hide the radio, which is exposed on the table. But he is too frightened, pressing himself flat against the wall in abject terror. The second example occurs at the end of the Act when the mocking Japanese voice is heard on the radio. Whitaker involuntarily rises from his seat in fear, having to be pushed back by Mitchem. The extreme nature of these responses points with tragic inevitability to his panic in Act 2, leading him to shoot the prisoner.

Whereas in Act 1 we learn much of Whitaker's character from stage directions which tell us what he does, in Act 2, he is given a more prominent speaking role as the playwright deepens his individuality. It is noticeable that it is to Smith, a fellow Tynesider, that he reveals the details of his personal life for he is assured of a sympathetic ear. These details – his pride in the watch he bought, his intention of giving it to his father as a present, his brief courtship of Mary Pearson – show him to be a simple, naive figure, uncertain whether at seventeen Mary is too young, and then sad that she has probably found someone else. However, any sympathy Whitaker arouses – and he generates a considerable amount in these conversations with Smith – must be viewed against his less sympathetic practice of buying war souvenirs looted from the Japanese dead. He evokes an ambiguous response, for he is both pitiable and wretched, so petrified of even the innocuous prisoner that he shoots him and thereby seals the fate of the entire patrol.

The Japanese Prisoner

He's almost human this one is

In many respects the prisoner is the principal character in the play, even though he never speaks. He is the most representative of all the characters, for he embodies the plight of the simple individual trapped by war, unable even to understand what his captors are saying. This last point is important, for the prisoner spends the entire play in ignorance. Unable to communicate verbally, he must rely on gestures, but these are often an inadequate alternative. The sudden change in Macleish's behaviour, for example, when Macleish accepts a cigarette from him only to assault him a few moments later must be bewildering to someone who has been unable to follow the argument about looting. He is important also in that simply by being Japanese he awakens differing responses in the patrol members, which clarify their characters – Johnstone's sadism, Bamforth's friendliness, Whitaker's terror and so on. Finally, of course, the moral integrity of every member of the patrol is measured by his attitude to the fate of the prisoner.

He is successfully individualized too, though, as with the other characters, this individuality emerges only gradually. He is the sole character to be described physically by the playwright, and this provides an important guide to Willis Hall's conception of him. Ridiculously over-armed, short, plump and frightened, he initially invites comparison with stereotyped characters from comic opera. His unheroic pathetic appearance is at odds with the weaponry he carries, and suggests that he presents no great threat to anyone as a soldier. From this unpromising beginning, he blossoms as a human being in his own right. His fear in the circumstances is quite understandable, as is his anxiety to please his captors. His simple pride in his family is conveyed when he shows Bamforth his photographs; more importantly this pride shows that he is part of a larger human family, sharing the same pleasures, fears and comforts as the men who wear a different uniform. Bamforth's roguish comment that the prisoner is as bad as Smudge (Smith) acknowledges this, for Smith and the prisoner are both family men.

As the play moves towards its violent end, the gestures of the prisoner, which reveal his essential similarity to his captors, become more poignant for we know that his fate has been decided. When, early in Act 2, the prisoner drinks from Mitchem's water bottle, he wipes the top after drinking in a rudimentary and universal act of good manners. Like Macleish and Evans, he is a smoker and so offers each of them a cigarette on separate occasions in Act 2. By the end, the patrol members, with the exception of Johnstone who hates him and Whitaker who is frightened of him, have established some kind of relationship with the prisoner, even if it is nothing more than offering and taking cigarettes, looking at photographs, giving him a drink of water. No one wants to kill him, discounting Johnstone. He has no wish to die a hero by making a daring attempt to escape or by warning his comrades of the patrol's presence in the hut. Yet despite this, a long burst from Whitaker's sten gun fills his body with bullets. His death shows the impersonal brutality at the heart of war.

Themes

Whereas the plot of a work of literature is the means by which the story is told, the themes are the ideas that concern the writer and with which he or she deals in the telling of the story. The major themes of *The Long and the Short and the Tall* – war, human dignity, responsibility and comradeship – are not presented as simple, one-sided issues by Willis Hall. There is no attempt to preach a message that can be reduced to an easy, straightforward summary of what the play is about. Although it reveals the horror and degradation of war, this is nothing so simple as an 'anti-war' propaganda play; it is all the more effective because of its refusal to take a one-sided attitude.

The single most important theme is war, from which the subordinate themes are derived. Until the capture of the Japanese soldier the inexperienced members of Mitchem's patrol have distorted and unrealistic views of what war is. They dislike it, of course, but their reasons for doing so are alarmingly naive. They resent it because it has meant their leaving their families and coming to an alien country for which they feel no personal affection or loyalty. Smith would rather be in his Tyneside council house with his wife and children, just as Evans would be happier at home in his Welsh valley. War has meant their joining the army, and army life is seen to be one of boring and oppressive routine: kit inspections, pointless patrols through the jungle, obedience to orders, lack of privacy in the barracks where tempers can easily explode, and poor food. These factors, all of which are features of war, make the cynicism of men like Bamforth immediately understandable, but they also point to the men's totally inadequate view of the nature of war. For them, it involves inconvenience but not much more than that. Insofar as they have ideas of what battle is like, these are woefully inadequate. Their barely concealed panic on hearing a Japanese voice over the radio is a stark reminder of their inexperience. Mitchem's scathing words a moment or two later reveal this. Half of them, he says, have been boasting of what they will do to the Japanese; their nervousness now reveals the emptiness of such boasts. To the personal inconvenience that war involves have been added danger and fear. There is worse to come, but before they are confronted with the real purpose of war, the theme is given a romantic, glamorous but also absurd presentation in the form of Evans's magazine story. In the world of romantic fiction, war and danger are linked with love and glory. The hero is, naturally, an officer, and of course is rather more special than merely a soldier; he is a hero, the kind of man who is posted on dangerous Special Missions undercover. Capture never ends in death, and in the traditional happy ending the officer gets both promotion and the girl. One has only to compare this fictional version with the fate of the patrol and the Japanese soldier.

It is only when Johnstone seizes the Japanese as he enters the hut and orders Evans to bayonet him that Mitchem's men come face to face with the reality of war. Personal discomfort, fear and danger are not its central feature: war is the systematic killing of one man by another by whatever means are available. With the exception of Bamforth, who is at first willing to kill the man, all the conscripts in the patrol recoil from this horrific reality. But this, as Mitchem tells Macleish in their conversation in Act 2, is precisely what war is like. This section of the play is central to Willis Hall's presentation of the theme, for it shows war to be degrading, brutalizing and stupid. Shakespeare's Othello speaks of the 'Pride, pomp and circumstance of glorious war', but such a chivalrous, idealized view is worlds away from Mitchem's more cynical beliefs. While he does not begrudge the men who win medals their glory for what are described as acts of valour, his description of them lays bare his attitude: 'square-head yobs who keep their brains between their legs'. They are the kind of people who, in Mitchem's view, stupidly disregard the danger they are in, survive their moment of folly, and are then called heroes and decorated. It is this romantic view of war people cherish, and which is the subject of glossy stories in magazines, but it is not representative of what war is really like. For Mitchem, the professional, war is mostly dirty, callous and unheroic – cold-bloodedly killing a man whom one does not hate, for instance. For this there is no glory and there are no medals.

In his treatment of the theme of war, then, Willis Hall has been savagely unheroic and unsentimental. Through Mitchem, valour is seen as mere hot-headedness; soldiers join the army not from any high-minded notions of serving king and country, but because their girlfriends think they would look smart in uniform. Most soldiers have little idea of what they are fighting for; death in battle is hardly heroic but may mean ending up with a hole in one's stomach. To give someone the fighting chance that Macleish believes in is nonsense because war is not a game but deadly conflict. This latter point is given its most ruthless treatment in the figure of Johnstone.

Of all the charactes in the play Johnstone is the least sympathetic, and yet he is the most consistent and the most realistic in his approach to war. Not in the least bothered by his conscience, Johnstone sees war simply as the extermination of the enemy and, failing that, their humiliation and degradation while they are prisoners. This is one of the most disturbing aspects of the play for it is impossible to dismiss this pitiless yet logical view. The primitive brutality of Johnstone is the perfect representation of the primitive brutality of war. In one respect, for war to have any rules of conduct is an absurdity – rules are an attempt to graft some kind of rational, civilized order on to behaviour that is irrational and barbaric. Rules of conduct might be appropriate for a game where one can lose and then start again, but the play makes clear that it is a misconception to see war in that way, for in war there is no second chance. So while we might find ourselves hostile to Johnstone's contempt for the Geneva Convention, and his subsequent treatment of the prisoner, we nonetheless have to realize that a humanitarian belief that war can be conducted in accordance with civilized principles is utterly at odds with the true but elemental nature of war embodied by Johnstone. To offer the enemy any kind of comfort is to sustain his morale; this then weakens one's own chance of winning. It is far simpler, and therefore more effective, to see the enemy as some kind of sub-species – hence Johnstone's telling, utterly contemptuous comment at the crisis of the play: 'It's a Jap!'

Yet despite being anti-heroic, the play is not a propaganda play that sees the subject from one side only. While it refuses to glamorize war, at no point does it suggest that wars can be avoided or human nature changed to make a more comfortable, secure world. It is this twist that makes the treatment of the theme both complex and realistic. Mitchem is used as the principal mouthpiece here in his conversation with Macleish in Act 2. Wars are inevitable because everyone is capable of killing. It is an integral part of human nature. The play does not merely state this theme: it actually shows it in action. Bamforth, finally the most highly principled of them all, would have killed the prisoner had not Mitchem stopped him; and Whitaker, who is the most nervous and cowardly patrol member, actually does kill him. Mitchem sadly recognizes that war is unavoidable and that he can do nothing to improve its conditions.

The other themes in the play are all seen in the context of the principal theme of war. One of the first casualties of conflict is human dignity. The play relentlessly shows the way in which war can quickly strip us of our illusions of ourselves as civilized human beings and reveal the violence, fear and selfishness that exist beneath. The Japanese soldier, for example, squirms in terror when he is first seized by Johnstone, and there are numerous occasions later when he cringes in fear. Such actions are hardly consistent with a notion of the human being as a dignified creature. Then there is his eagerness to please his captors by performing tricks to Bamforth's instructions. At the very end of Act 1 he is under the misapprehension that he is expected to entertain them, and so dutifully puts his hands on his head and looks for their approval. While this might be superficially comic, it is a fundamentally pathetic gesture: it demonstrates clearly that he is quite willing to behave more like a performing animal than a human being if it will save his life.

Yet he is not alone in finding himself acting in a base manner. Macleish professes belief in the Geneva Convention, at the very heart of which is the notion that even in war there are certain aspects of human dignity that should be respected. Yet over the issue of the British cigarette, his ideals are shown to be rooted in very shallow soil. His rage at the notion of looting is fanned by the very natural concern he feels for his brother, and leads him to declare violently that he will kill the prisoner. Later, he even refuses to look Bamforth in the eye when asked for his support, but stares out of the window saying nothing. Of the other conscripts, Evans, Smith and Whitaker are shown to be ordinary men whose basic selfishness and fear are exposed in the crucible of war. Faced with letting the prisoner live and thereby endangering their own lives, or having him killed, they choose the latter. Each puts forward his reasons: Smith that he, too, has a family who rely on him; Evans, more lamely when taxed by Bamforth, that perhaps the prisoner is a looter after all; Whitaker, whom the occasion strips of every vestige of dignity, who says initially that the patrol must get back and then blurts out the selfish but true reason, 'I've got to get back!' Moments later it is the wretched Whitaker who screams in abject terror in the jungle and dies calling for his mother.

As the unfolding events of the play have shown, none of these men is evil. Evans and Macleish have even made some human contact with the prisoner. However, under stress they shed their human decency and are willing to sacrifice another human being in order to save themselves. Yet it is hard to apportion blame. Obviously, in comparison with Bamforth, they suffer. We might disapprove of what they do, but it is completely understandable. War, which brings out a hitherto unknown fineness in Bamforth, is equally capable of revealing human selfishness. People act according to their notions of responsibility.

Throughout the play, the theme of *responsibility* is presented in a variety of ways. In Act 1, Macleish solemnly announces that having accepted the rank of lance corporal he now has a duty to support his fellow NCOs and therefore cannot allow the men in his charge to speak disrespectfully of Johnstone. As we shall see later, Macleish's conversation with Mitchem in Act 2 makes him uncomfortably aware that responsibility involves rather more than the simple maintenance of discipline. Later in the same Act, Bamforth informs Evans and Smith that at the prospect of any danger he will disguise himself and flee. It is quite a comic account, but reveals that at this stage Bamforth believes his sole responsibility is to save himself. This contrasts with Mitchem's wider idea of responsibility. Initially, he wants the prisoner taken back to base because of the information he might be able to give about the Japanese strength. In other words, he feels a duty to the army at large. More immediately, his duty is to the men who make up his patrol. If the prisoner becomes an obstacle to them he will kill him. As he tells Johnstone in Act 1, 'I've got six men. They're my responsibility.' Mitchem realizes that responsibility brings with it the necessity to make cruel decisions, and he accepts this though he does not like it. Macleish, on the other hand, has to be brought face to face with this uncomfortable fact. Appalled by the news that the prisoner is to be killed, Macleish says early in Act 2 that he does not care if he is stripped of his lance corporal's tape. Mitchem immediately realizes that what Macleish wishes is freedom from the burden of responsibility that the tape represents.

It is in the closing moments of the play that the theme of responsibility is explored most intensely and most variously. Mitchem, reluctantly but consistently, is willing to sacrifice the prisoner to save the others. It is significant that his words to Bamforth concern his men, not himself: 'it's all these lads or him.' In other words, right to the end he accepts the responsibility his rank imposes. Smith's duty is to his wife and children, Whitaker's solely to himself. Each of these characters presents differing versions of the theme. Overriding them all is Bamforth. It is Bamforth who insists on the human dignity of the prisoner with his simple but compelling retort that he too is a man. It is Bamforth who sees that they have a responsibility they cannot evade, as Smith wishes when he asks to be left out of it. In Bamforth, the theme of responsibility achieves a universal significance for it transcends group loyalty and race to enfold the responsibility each human being must accept for the welfare of another.

This does not mean that we accept Bamforth's version to the exclusion of the others. One of the deliberately uncomfortable aspects of the play is that it refuses to offer clear-cut, neatly formulated choices. Although Mitchem's concern for his men represents a narrower vision of the concept of responsibility than Bamforth's, it can be neither ignored nor dismissed for it is perfectly valid and honourably consistent. What Willis Hall does in his treatment of this theme is to make us face an acute moral problem while he dramatizes different responses to it. It is clear enough which is the most admirable, but he does not claim that it is exclusively the right one. The play would be less unsettling and therefore less successful if he did.

So far we have looked at the themes that shape the tragic mood of the play, but if war often demeans human dignity and pushes most people towards a selfish idea of what constitutes responsibility, it does have its positive side. The communal life the men lead, which can so easily lead to friction, also brings them together in *comradeship*. This can take a variety of forms. In the first Act, much of the banter of Evans and Bamforth is reminiscent of schoolboy high spirits and they even spar playfully with each other. There is the amusement of Smith and Bamforth as Evans relates the preposterous incidents in his magazine story. There is, too, the constant opportunity to complain to one's fellows about the awfulness of life in the army. On the gentler, more reflective side, the chance is there to find relief by speaking into a sympathetic ear of one's private yearnings and fears. Whitaker does this twice with Smith in Act 2, and Smith himself speaks to Evans of his home life and is listened to with understanding. Naturally, tempers often flare and the men react violently to each other, but these moments of comradeship are revealing and should not be ignored.

Language and style

When he saw the play performed in 1959 the theatre critic Kenneth Tynan wrote enthusiastically that each character

> ... speaks a language so abundant in racy local metaphor that I could have kicked myself for having acquiesced in the popular myth that British vernacular is dull whenever it is not Americanized. Mr Hall's play is not only boisterous, exuberant and accurate; it is also beautifully written. (See p. 70).

Given that so much of the language consists of slang expressions, Tynan's last comment might seem to be wide of the mark, for we hardly connect slang with beautiful writing. Yet he is quite right for in its way *The Long and the Short and the Tall* is a triumph of style. The language is so racy, so sure in its colloquial tone that we never doubt we are listening to an exact representation of the way ordinary people speak. The language and style, then, impress and convince us of the realism of the characters. We recognize that as uneducated men they are not capable of profound, sophisticated utterances, though what they lack in subtlety they make up for in vigour. When the language does become more sophisticated, particularly on the occasion when Macleish expresses loyalty to his fellow NCOs, the intention is to show how alien such a form of speech generally is to him. Instead of sounding dignified he is merely pompous.

As a feature of speech the *slang* in the play has two advantages over standard English: firstly, it reinforces group identity; secondly, its colourful expressions mirror precisely the social class of the characters. There is not, surprisingly, a great deal of army slang in the play. Soldiers, like other groups of people, inevitably develop a form of language understood within their circle but not necessarily outside it. Single words such as 'stag', 'tapes', 'mob', 'spout' and 'ticks' are instantly understood by the patrol members to mean 'sentry duty', 'chevrons', 'military unit', 'rifle breech' and 'complaints', though these meanings are not immediately clear to anyone outside the army. Given that the British Army has fought in all parts of the world, it is hardly surprising that its slang reflects this breadth of experience; Bamforth, for instance, a Londoner through and through, uses quite naturally 'doolally', 'Bungy', 'wallahs' and 'Blighty', which are Indian in origin.

The second feature of slang is that it can reflect accurately the social class of the speaker. As Willis Hall is concerned with the behaviour of ordinary uneducated men it is essential for the authenticity of the play that their language be consistent with their background. Slang is often a vague form of expression used by people who do not have the vocabulary to say precisely what they mean. It provides them with ready-made words and phrases, which they can use again and again on appropriate occasions. This sometimes means that what the characters say depends for its meaning on the tone of voice and the context in which it is said rather then the actual words used, as in the use of the words 'carve up'. Bamforth first uses it to mean 'beaten up' and possibly slashed with a razor when speaking of London street fighters. Later he tells Evans that what is happening in England is a 'carve up', in the sense that it is crooked; later still he says that he hopes Macleish's brother is 'carved up', meaning killed. The phrase 'knock off' also depends on context or tone to make its meaning clear; when Bamforth and Evans tussle in Act 1 Macleish orders them to 'knock it off', meaning to stop. Later in Act 1 Johnstone tells Mitchem that they should take the prisoner outside and 'knock him off', meaning kill him. Early in Act 2 Whitaker tells Smith that the watch he bought had been 'knocked off', meaning stolen. These are not the only occasions when the same phrases can have different shades of meaning in different contexts, but whenever they occur, they are clearly understood by the other members of the patrol. Their presence in the play reveals Willis Hall's keen ear for the way in which ordinary people actually speak, often rather imprecisely, relying on their tone of voice to convey their meaning. His success lies in the way he makes us believe we are listening to a transcript from life.

Although slang is often characterized by its vagueness it can also strike us by its vigour and its coarseness: Mitchem's words to Macleish that there could have been 'seven men with their tripes on the floor' creates a powerful and unpleasant visual image. Evans's observation that the Japanese soldier is a 'skiving get' has a much more graphic effect than its standard English equivalent. Similarly, to have 'the screaming ab-dabs' paints a far more colourful picture than the more restrained to have 'a bout of hysterics'.

Of all the characters in the play it is Bamforth, the cockney, whose speech reveals the most obvious regional characteristics, especially in his use of rhyming slang. A feature worth noticing is the way in which the patrol members occasionally show how their speech has been influenced by contact with men from different parts of the country.

Thus, at times, Evans and Whitaker both use cockney rhyming slang terms.

The language does not rely solely on its vocabulary for its truth to life. How the words are linked together to express ideas is as important as individual words in making the dialogue realistic. Most of the speeches are brief, indicating the men's general unease with language, Bamforth and, to an extent, Mitchem excepted. Ideas are usually expressed in short sentences, for casual speech is often spoken in a kind of shorthand. Mitchem's words in Act 1 shortly before he and Johnstone leave the hut illustrate this: 'Better stay inside. Don't show yourselves. Cover the front . . .' The play abounds with examples of this kind of utterance, revealing the men's inability to formulate complex sentences to express their thoughts.

Sometimes, though, the inadequacy of their language can be moving. Smith describing his home, and Whitaker talking of Mary Pearson, for example, are instances of inarticulate men speaking touchingly of matters that affect them deeply.

Dramatic structure

From the time that Johnstone kicks in the door of the hut and appears menacingly with a sten gun at his hip, until we hear the agonized death cries of the patrol and Johnstone re-enters wounded and bleeding, the play is a compelling mixture of humour, poignancy and high drama. Given the realism of the characters and the convincing mixture of colloquialism and slang that they speak, it is easy to see the play as presenting a graphic but recognizable slice of life rather than a tightly structured work of art. It is, of course, the playwright's intention that we should see both characters and action as realistic, but it is worth pausing for a moment to consider what realism means in the theatre. Put simply, it is the belief that what happens on stage should be as true to life as possible; that is, the plot should not be far-fetched, the characters should be recognizable in ordinary life and the language should convince by its authenticity. But while doing this might make a play seem realistic, it would not necessarily make it interesting. The writer must also carefully select and arrange material, highlight some events rather than others, offer character contrasts, clashes of interest, changes of tone, and give a sense of shape to the action so as to provide the audience with a satisfactory dramatic experience. Realism in the theatre, then, is often achieved by unrealistic artistic methods. Willis Hall manipulates his material in this realistic play just as surely as someone like Samuel Beckett does in an 'unrealistic' play like *Happy Days* in which the main character spends the entire time buried up to her waist in sand. But they do so for different purposes: Willis Hall to heighten the drama by showing how 'real' people behave under stress; Samuel Beckett to show how life traps people, and how pointless is human aspiration. Hall's play, then, seeks to present the audience with the impression of realism, not the thing itself. No play can do that.

The Long and the Short and the Tall is an excellent example of a work that seems to be drawn straight from life but has, in fact, been very carefully contrived and structured to work in dramatic terms. As an example of the shaping hand of the writer one has only to look at the very beginning and end of the play. Balanced against each other they provide a pleasing symmetry for the audience, as well as imposing a clear structural pattern. The action of the play begins off-stage with gunfire, the birdsong and the dramatic appearance of Johnstone in the doorway. Silence, gunfire and jungle noises alternate, each serving to emphasize the other. It closes with the death of the men off-stage; Johnstone reappearing, slamming shut the door he had kicked open at the beginning; and the contrast between the burst from the Japanese machine-gun and the silence that follows. The play closes with the bird singing in the jungle. These incidents, so carefully echoing one another, have been consciously selected and highlighted by the writer to enrich the dramatic effect and contrast the violence of the action with the peace of nature and its indifference to human affairs.

Further evidence of the control exercised by Willis Hall is there within the events of the play itself. In its construction it closely follows the classical model, something which might appear odd in a play that is so 'realistic'. Two thousand three hundred years ago the Greek philosopher Aristotle noted that the greatest Greek tragedies followed what have since become known as the Dramatic Unities of time, place and action. That is, in these plays the timescale was roughly equivalent to the time the events would actually take to occur in normal life; there was only one setting; and there was no sub-plot. It is immediately obvious how *The Long and the Short and the Tall* subscribes to this classical model: the play begins in the late afternoon and ends in the early evening with only a thirty-minute gap between the close of Act 1 and the opening of Act 2; apart from the cries of the dying men at the end, the action takes place within the confines of the hut; and the plot deals exclusively with the attitudes of the men towards one another and towards the prisoner. The plays of which Aristotle wrote, such as *Oedipus Rex* and *Antigone*, are highly formalized, unrealistic in that they tell of mythical heroes and heroines, but the classical Dramatic Unities themselves need not be seen as dry and remote from modern theatre; they can offer playwrights twofold benefits. Firstly, they can generate immense dramatic intensity, and the dramatic intensity which is there in Greek tragedy is still readily available to modern playwrights. Once the play begins there is nothing to distract the audience from the relentless unfolding of events: there are no interruptions for scene changes, no diverting sub-plots to distract the attention from the main concern of the play, and no adjustments to make in the timescale. Secondly, although they do not do so in Greek tragedy, the three Unities can actually enhance the feeling of realism in a play, for the action occurs under the same circumstances that it would in real life. No imaginative leaps through space or time are required. We do not, as in Shakespeare's *Antony and Cleopatra*, have to move rapidly between Rome, Egypt and other settings in the ancient world, nor are we called upon, as we are in *The Winter's Tale*, also by Shakespeare, to imagine half-way through the play that sixteen years have passed.

However, the benefits gained by imposing these severe limits upon the time, place and action of a play can lead to disaster if there is not enough variety and dynamism within characters and narrative to stimulate the interest of the audience and keep it stimulated by offering exciting yet plausible developments. Willis Hall carefully ensures that his play has these requisite qualities. The overall construction of the play is simple yet dramatically effective. There are two Acts, both of which follow the same broad structural pattern: rising tension offset by moments of relaxation achieved through humour or reflection. Each Act culminates in a moment of dramatic excitement, first when the mocking Japanese voice is heard at the end of Act 1 and second when the prisoner and most of the patrol are killed at the end of Act 2.

Yet Act 2 is no mere duplication of Act 1 for its tone is more consistently sombre. Careful reading of the first Act will show that the tension is constantly being increased and then lowered, usually by comedy or at least humour, until the final climactic moment. The potentially violent clash between Johnstone and Bamforth at the outset gives way to Bamforth's cheeky humour and the more personal reflections of Smith and Evans when Johnstone and Mitchem are on reconnaissance outside. This in turn gives way to the ugly encounter between Bamforth and Macleish; a still further rise in excitement generated by the grave implications of the Japanese voice on the radio; then the actual sighting of the Japanese soldier. But even this latter moment of tension is leavened by humour as Bamforth laughs at the soldier having a quiet cigarette. The drama of the prisoner's capture, seemingly certain death, and reprieve by Mitchem, give way to greater relaxation when Bamforth amuses himself by giving him a series of comic instructions – though even this is punctuated by Bamforth's attack on Johnstone. Matters become even more serious when Smith and Macleish return with news that the Japanese forces have broken through the front line in strength. Their imminent danger is underlined by the eerie broken English of a Japanese voice, which startles them all at the close of the Act.

In Act 2 the humour is largely, though not entirely, replaced by reflective conversations, which provide dramatic contrast to the moments of excitement and tension. Given the desperate plight of Mitchem's patrol it is only to be expected that there are fewer moments of dramatic relaxation than there were in Act 1: their chances of escape are understood to be minimal and the best they can expect is to become prisoners of war. Still, two major occasions for contrast are provided. The first comes right at the beginning of the Act. This is a skilful piece of construction, for from this quiet moment between Smith and Whitaker, Willis Hall can gradually tighten the intensity of the action. It begins to rise during the disagreement between Mitchem and Macleish, and is continued when Johnstone and Mitchem discuss who shall kill the prisoner and the marked difference between the two men then becomes apparent. This part of the Act reaches its peak when the prisoner is suspected of looting and the pent-up anxieties of the men find temporary release in their bitter accusations. There follows a brief humorous moment when Evans changes guard with exaggerated smartness. Thereafter, Whitaker is further used by Willis Hall to introduce a softer, more reflective tone when he tells Smith of his courtship of Mary Pearson. Then there is a dramatic rise in tension once more as the play moves swiftly to its dreadful and final climax.

Running beneath both Acts as a feature of their dramatic structure is the use made by Willis Hall of *conflict*. In the first half of Act 1 the conflict exists among the patrol members themselves, for on this routine patrol they feel little initial threat from the enemy. This conflict within the group takes a variety of forms. There is the personal dislike Johnstone and Bamforth feel for each other which is actually expressed in physical violence at one point. Then there is Macleish's anger at Bamforth which stops short of their fighting only because Smith intercedes. Less violent, but just as important, is Whitaker's dislike of Bamforth's jokes about him, a dislike made all the more ominous because they are true. To this can be added Mitchem's fury when he and Johnstone return to find no sentries on guard. His anger at Macleish, Bamforth, and the men in general is another graphic example of the rifts within the patrol. So far the conflict has been localized within the hut and among the men themselves. The arrival of the prisoner allows their differing attitudes to be more sharply focused.

As the play proceeds, however, the notion of conflict acquires a larger context. Mitchem's men, so often divided among themselves, have to face the growing threat from what is outside in the jungle. Mitchem's hope that the prisoner is a member of a small patrol vanishes when Smith and Macleish return with their grim news. So, as well as the more immediately perceived group conflict, which can and does occur as a consequence of discord within the group, there is increasingly the larger, external menace, all the more frightening because it is not seen. In fact, one can see how the play is constructed to show that the friction within the patrol leads directly to their coming into violent conflict with the Japanese soldiers who kill them.

One of the most satisfying features of the structure is the use of *contrasts* and *parallels*, which allows Willis Hall to enrich the texture of the play. They occur in both character and situation. Perhaps the two most memorably theatrical situations in the play are built upon parallels and contrasts, one occurring in each Act. Bamforth's defence of the prisoner's life in Act 2 would lose much of its potency if it were not for the moment in Act 1 when the prisoner is also threatened. As Johnstone holds the struggling man, first Evans, then Macleish and then Smith are ordered to kill him. In moments of growing tension, none of them can do it. Finally, Bamforth says callously that it is the same as carving a pig and takes the bayonet from Evans. So Bamforth is differentiated here from the other conscripts. In Act 2, there is a parallel moment when once more the prisoner faces death. Bamforth is again distinguished from the others but this time because of his vehement defence of the prisoner. In precisely the same way that Johnstone went from man to man ordering them to kill the Japanese, so Bamforth now goes from man to man asking them to support him in saving the man's life. The one situation uncannily parallels yet contrasts with the other. This dramatic moment gains its raw power from the complete reversal of attitudes that has taken place between the two incidents and shows how far the characters have developed in response to the events of the play.

However, contrasts and parallels occur not only in terms of the dramatic action; the characters themselves are the subject of the same balancing and contrasting. Some of them are obvious – the naive Evans and the know-all Bamforth; the brutal Johnstone and the more restrained Mitchem; the talkative Bamforth and the taciturn Smith; the conscientious Whitaker and the idle Bamforth, and so on. It is by constantly allowing us to judge one character in the light of another that each personality comes into clearer, more identifiable focus. There are, too, the contrasts existing not only between characters but within characters themselves. Thus Bamforth acts at the end in precisely the opposite way from what, in Act 1, he says he will do. Macleish abandons his early belief in the importance of the Geneva

Convention; Mitchem, who tells Johnstone bluntly that he will kill the Japanese himself if necessary, is clearly reluctant to do so and even tells Macleish that he has considered binding him and leaving him. There are occasions also when the least expected characters parallel each other quite suddenly making us see similarities where none were obvious before. Bamforth's humorous remark in Act 1 that the prisoner is as bad as Smith has the startling effect of yoking together two men who have nothing in common except that they have wives and children. But this is precisely Willis Hall's point, for it gives them a shared personal experience of a kind that no one else on stage possesses. More subtly, there is that telling moment already referred to when we examined Mitchem's character, when he twice tells Bamforth that he is sorry but the prisoner must die. These two men who have provided a consistently sharp contrast in their attitudes throughout the play are momentarily paralleled as men with deep but incompatible responsibilities.

General questions

1 How does Willis Hall present the character of Whitaker and how does he intend us to feel towards him?

Guideline notes

His diligence and conscientiousness evident from the start. Begins operating the radio as soon as he enters hut. Says very little in Act 1, but character presented through his actions – darning socks for Saturday inspection, for example – and others' opinions of him. Bamforth ridicules both his acceptance of army discipline and his nervous disposition. At this stage, we see Whitaker as the raw recruit, someone who is less disillusioned than the others. We feel sympathy for him when Johnstone implies that he is inefficient, for Whitaker is the only enlisted man present who has been serious about what he does. Nervousness increasingly evident in second half of Act 1; he stares horrified at the radio when he hears Japanese voice, is paralysed with fear in a moment of crisis and cannot hide the radio, and is further terrified when hears broken English of Japanese radio operator.

Given a larger speaking role in Act 2 so that individuality can be developed. First action in Act 2, however, is to start in fear when hears a bird singing. His gullibility and simplicity made evident in conversation with Smith; it is clear he had been overcharged for watch, and seems to think it was both Peruvian and Siamese. Once more, sympathy evoked for Whitaker here. However, Willis Hall at pains not to present Whitaker as consistently sympathetic. Less attractive side emerges when Bamforth exposes his hobby of collecting war trophies. Unwilling to admit it at first. If Bamforth to be believed, Whitaker will take trophies home and boast of his war exploits. Extreme nervousness once again referred to by Bamforth here, and evident later in his giving the prisoner a wide berth.

Character softened once more in second talk with Smith. His obvious affection for Mary Pearson touchingly shown as is his suspicion that she has now found someone else. During climax of the play becomes a pathetic figure, selfish and panic-stricken.

Shoots the prisoner in abject fear and dies screaming, vivid reminder by Willis Hall that war is not glorious and most soldiers not heroes. Our attitudes towards Whitaker change during the play from sympathy to contempt, yet it is impossible not to feel deep regret that someone so inexperienced and pathetic meets the fate he does.

2 What do you think of Sergeant Mitchem? You might wish to consider some of these points while thinking of your answer:
    how he acts as leader of the patrol;
    his behaviour towards the prisoner;
    what he says in his conversation with Macleish early in Act 2;
    any ways in which he is different from Johnstone.

3 How important is what we are told of the characters' background to our understanding of them?

4 Consider the various ways in which the theme of responsibility is presented in the play.

5 Do you find yourself liking Bamforth unreservedly? Here are some points you might wish to consider while thinking of your answer:
    his aggressive attitude towards Macleish;
    his mockery of Whitaker;
    his humorous 'Margaret Denning' letter;
    his attempts to converse with the Japanese soldier;
    his defence of the soldier against the charge of looting;
    his defence of the soldier's life.

6 Re-read the opening of the play from the time Johnstone first speaks until a fight between Bamforth and himself is prevented by Mitchem. Then answer these questions:
    (a) How is Bamforth's anti-authority attitude revealed?
    (b) What does this extract tell you about Mitchem?
    (c) In what ways are Mitchem and Johnstone differentiated?

7 What are your feelings towards the Japanese prisoner? Consider some of these points for your answer:
    his appearance;
    his treatment by Johnstone;
    his fear of death;
    his relationship with Bamforth;
    his willingness to please;
    his family.

8 What does the play gain by having the action take place within a confined space and time?

9 One of the most noticeable features of the play is its reliance upon slang. How does this add to the impression of realism?

10 Imagine that Johnstone is being questioned by the Japanese. He has been asked to give a brief account of what has happened. Because he despises the Japanese, he considers it below his dignity to lie. What do you think he would say? While you are thinking of your answer, you might wish to consider these points:
  Johnstone wanted the prisoner killed immediately he was captured;
  Mitchem believed the prisoner could provide valuable information;
  Bamforth and Macleish (to a lesser extent) strike up a relationship with the prisoner;
  Johnstone's attitude towards the prisoner over the matter of the photographs and the British cigarette.

11 Re-read the section from the climax of the play in Act 2, from the point where Mitchem tells Bamforth that they will need every drop of water for themselves because the Japanese will be at every water hole, to where he orders Bamforth to get to one side, and then answer these questions:
  (a) How do the stage directions help the reader to follow what is happening?
  (b) What do we learn of Mitchem from this extract?
  (c) Is Mitchem's attitude towards Bamforth here typical of his attitude elsewhere? Give some examples from the rest of the play.

12 How do the stage directions help someone who is reading the play (rather than seeing it performed) to understand fully what is happening? Try to give some specific examples of occasions where they clarified or deepened your understanding.

13 Discuss the way in which the relationship between Bamforth and Evans has changed by the time Bamforth stands up for the prisoner.

14 Willis Hall has stated that the play is about human dignity. Consider the way in which it deals with this concept.

General questions

15 Re-read the section in Act 2, from the point where Mitchem tells Macleish that war is not like a game of darts down to where Mitchem mentions Rudolph Valentino, and then answer these questions:
  (a) What is Mitchem's attitude to war as it is expressed here?
  (b) What is his attitude towards women?
  (c) In this extract how, and why, does Macleish's attitude change?

16 What is Smith's role in the play?

17 Do you think that the play is an anti-war play?

18 Show how effectively the play rises and falls in tension by selecting and discussing two or three examples.

19 What are your views of Macleish?

20 Try to account for the lasting popularity of the play.

Further reading

There are no books currently in print dealing exclusively with Willis Hall. However, those listed below either include some discussion of *The Long and the Short and the Tall* or give valuable background detail on the theatre of the 1950s, which will help to deepen one's appreciation of the play.

At the Royal Court, edited by Richard Findlater (Amber Lane Press, 1981)
A View of the English Stage 1944–1963, Kenneth Tynan (Davis-Poynter, 1975)
British Theatre 1950/70, Arnold Hinchliffe (Basil Blackwell, 1974)
The Modern Writer and his World, G. S. Fraser (Pelican Books, 1972)
Mid-Century Drama, Laurence Kitchen (Faber, 1960)

Notes

Notes

Notes

Notes

Notes

Titles published in the Brodie's Notes series

W. H. Auden Selected Poetry

Jane Austen Emma Mansfield Park Northanger Abbey Persuasion Pride and Prejudice

Anthologies of Poetry Ten Twentieth Century Poets The Poet's Tale The Metaphysical Poets

Samuel Beckett Waiting for Godot

Arnold Bennett The Old Wives' Tale

William Blake Songs of Innocence and Experience

Robert Bolt A Man for All Seasons

Harold Brighouse Hobson's Choice

Charlotte Brontë Jane Eyre

Emily Brontë Wuthering Heights

Robert Browning Selected Poetry

John Bunyan The Pilgrim's Progress

Geoffrey Chaucer (parallel texts editions) The Franklin's Tale The Knight's Tale The Miller's Tale The Nun's Priest's Tale The Pardoner's Tale Prologue to the Canterbury Tales The Wife of Bath's Tale

John Clare Selected Poetry and Prose

Samuel Taylor Coleridge Selected Poetry and Prose

Wilkie Collins The Woman in White

William Congreve The Way of the World

Joseph Conrad Heart of Darkness The Nigger of the Narcissus & Youth The Secret Agent

Charles Dickens Bleak House David Copperfield Dombey and Son Great Expectations Hard Times Little Dorrit Oliver Twist Our Mutual Friend A Tale of Two Cities

Gerald Durrell My Family and Other Animals

George Eliot Middlemarch The Mill on the Floss Silas Marner

T. S. Eliot Murder in the Cathedral Selected Poems

J. G. Farrell The Siege of Krishnapur

Titles published in the Brodie's Notes series 77

W. Faulkner As I Lay Dying

Henry Fielding Joseph Andrews Tom Jones

F. Scott Fitzgerald The Great Gatsby

E. M. Forster Howards End A Passage to India
Where Angels Fear to Tread

William Golding Lord of the Flies The Spire

Oliver Goldsmith She Stoops to Conquer

Graham Greene Brighton Rock The Power and the Glory
The Quiet American The Human Factor

Thom Gunn and Ted Hughes Selected Poems

Thomas Hardy Chosen Poems of Thomas Hardy
Far from the Madding Crowd Jude the Obscure
The Mayor of Casterbridge Return of the Native
Tess of the d'Urbervilles The Trumpet-Major The Woodlanders

L. P. Hartley The Go-Between The Shrimp and the Anemone

Joseph Heller Catch-22

Ernest Hemingway A Farewell to Arms For Whom the Bell Tolls
The Old Man and the Sea

Barry Hines A Kestrel for a Knave

Gerard Manley Hopkins Poetry and Prose of Gerard Manley Hopkins

Henry James Washington Square

Ben Jonson The Alchemist Volpone

James Joyce A Portrait of the Artist as a Young Man Dubliners

John Keats Selected Poems and Letters of John Keats

Ken Kesey One Flew over the Cuckoo's Nest

Rudyard Kipling Kim

D. H. Lawrence The Rainbow Selected Tales Sons and Lovers

Harper Lee To Kill a Mockingbird

Laurie Lee As I Walked out One Midsummer Morning
Cider with Rosie

Thomas Mann Death in Venice Tonio Kröger

Christopher Marlowe Doctor Faustus Edward the Second

W. Somerset Maugham Of Human Bondage

Gavin Maxwell Ring of Bright Water

The Long and the Short and the Tall

Thomas Middleton The Changeling

Arthur Miller The Crucible Death of a Salesman

John Milton A Choice of Milton's Verse Comus and Samson Agonistes Paradise Lost I, II

Sean O'Casey Juno and the Paycock
The Shadow of a Gunman and the Plough and the Stars

George Orwell Animal Farm 1984

John Osborne Luther

Alexander Pope Selected Poetry

J. B. Priestley An Inspector Calls

J. D. Salinger The Catcher in the Rye

Siegfried Sassoon Memoirs of a Fox-Hunting Man

Peter Shaffer The Royal Hunt of the Sun

William Shakespeare Antony and Cleopatra As You Like It
Coriolanus Hamlet Henry IV (Part I) Henry IV (Part II)
Henry V Julius Caesar King Lear Love's Labour's Lost
Macbeth Measure for Measure The Merchant of Venice
A Midsummer Night's Dream Much Ado about Nothing
Othello Richard II Richard III Romeo and Juliet The Sonnets
The Taming of the Shrew The Tempest Twelfth Night
The Winter's Tale

G. B. Shaw Androcles and the Lion Arms and the Man
Caesar and Cleopatra The Doctor's Dilemma Pygmalion Saint Joan

Richard Sheridan Plays of Sheridan: The Rivals; The Critic;
The School for Scandal

John Steinbeck The Grapes of Wrath Of Mice and Men & The Pearl

Tom Stoppard Rosencrantz and Guildenstern are Dead

J. M. Synge The Playboy of the Western World

Jonathan Swift Gulliver's Travels

Alfred Tennyson Selected Poetry

William Thackeray Vanity Fair

Flora Thompson Lark Rise to Candleford

Dylan Thomas Under Milk Wood

Anthony Trollope Barchester Towers

Mark Twain Huckleberry Finn

Keith Waterhouse Billy Liar

Evelyn Waugh Decline and Fall Scoop
H. G. Wells The History of Mr Polly The War of the Worlds
John Webster The Duchess of Malfi The White Devil
Oscar Wilde The Importance of Being Earnest
Virginia Woolf To the Lighthouse
William Wordsworth The Prelude (Books 1, 2)
William Wycherley The Country Wife
W. B. Yeats Selected Poetry
GCSE English coursework: Prose G. Handley and P. Wilkins
GCSE English coursework: Drama and Poetry K. Dowling

All Pan books are available at your local bookshop or newsagent, or can be ordered direct from the publisher. Indicate the number of copies required and fill in the form below.

Send to: **CS Department, Pan Books Ltd., P.O. Box 40,
Basingstoke, Hants.   RG21 2YT.**

or phone: 0256 469551 (Ansaphone), quoting title, author and Credit Card number.

Please enclose a remittance* to the value of the cover price plus: 60p for the first book plus 30p per copy for each additional book ordered to a maximum charge of £2.40 to cover postage and packing.

*Payment may be made in sterling by UK personal cheque, postal order, sterling draft or international money order, made payable to Pan Books Ltd.

Alternatively by Barclaycard/Access:

Card No. ☐☐☐☐☐☐☐☐☐☐☐☐☐☐☐☐

Signature:

Applicable only in the UK and Republic of Ireland.

While every effort is made to keep prices low, it is sometimes necessary to increase prices at short notice. Pan Books reserve the right to show on covers and charge new retail prices which may differ from those advertised in the text or elsewhere.

NAME AND ADDRESS IN BLOCK LETTERS PLEASE:

....

Name———————————————————————————

Address———————————————————————————

3/87